Tube Ritual

TUBE RITUAL

JUMP-START YOUR JOURNEY TO 5,000 YOUTUBE SUBSCRIBERS

BRIAN G. JOHNSON

NEW YORK

LONDON • NASHVILLE • MELBOURNE • VANCOUVER

Tube Ritual

Jumpstart Your Journey to 5,000 YouTube Subscribers

Published in New York, New York, by Morgan James Publishing. Morgan James is a trademark of Morgan James, LLC. www.MorganJamesPublishing.com

The Morgan James Speakers Group can bring authors to your live event. For more information or to book an event visit The Morgan James Speakers Group at www.TheMorganJamesSpeakersGroup.com.

ISBN 9781642790184 paperback
ISBN 9781642790191 eBook
Library of Congress Control Number: 2018936962

Cover Design by:
Matt Clark
ImageDesigns.com

Cover Photo by:
Teresa Lee
TeresaLeePhotography.com

Interior Design by:
Chris Treccani
www.3dogcreative.net

In an effort to support local communities, raise awareness and funds, Morgan James Publishing donates a percentage of all book sales for the life of each book to Habitat for Humanity Peninsula and Greater Williamsburg.

Get involved today! Visit
www.MorganJamesBuilds.com

CONTENTS

ACKNOWLEDGMENTS

First and foremost, thanks to my amazing wife, Amanda. I love you and our life together. We've got it pretty darn good if I do say so myself! Thanks to Joel Comm and Colin Theriot for dropping hints that resulted in me digging deep into this thing called "YouTube."

Thanks to Kevin Knebl for spreading kindness, something I believe this world could use a bit more of. Thanks to Tim Schmoyer for not just sharing solid information on YouTube, but providing detailed information that greatly impacted this book. Thanks to my buddy and YouTuber extraordinaire, Nick Nimmin. Thanks to Owen Hemsath for coining the phrase "Win the Click" and for being an inspiration to so many. Thanks to Dan Brock, The Deadbeat Super Affiliate, for reaching out about doing a video collaboration. Watching you fly on YouTube has been very cool, my friend.

For those who have come before me and shared the YouTube and video how-to goodness, thank you. This includes Sean Cannell, Herman Drost, Lon Naylor, Lou Bortone, Amy Schmittauer, and Sunny "Stay in Your Lane" Lenarduzzi.

To Roberto Blake, David Walsh, Derral Eves, and Steve Dotto, thanks for setting the bar so high for the rest of us.

Matthew Gielen, thanks for providing your thoughts and insights on YouTube SEO. Matt Clark, you sir, have the creative chops of the graphic gods, and I love what we have come up with together. Jamus

McKenna, thanks for keeping me in your thoughts. If not for you, I would not have appeared on James Schramko's super-fancy podcast and website!

To Felicia Slattery and Anthony Prichard, you're both amazing role models and I dig your hustle. Well done! Last, this acknowledgment section would not be complete without mentioning some of the amazing people who make the **Tube Ritual Facebook Group** what it is.

A big B-to-the-G thank you to: Tim Knox, Steve Gamlin, Cricket Wilson Harris, Brandon Nankivell, Dale L. Roberts, Andy Simpson, Naomi Skarzinski, Gene Pimentel, Jessica Miller Stapleton, Benali Amine, Bertram Health Sr., Ben Shaffer, Peter Nez, Rex Harris, Gord Isman, Tracy Malone, Patel King, Michael Akers, Kurt Melvin, Shane Vozar, Paul Irvine, and all the members of the Tube Ritual Facebook Group.

INTRODUCTION

In July 2016, it started to get just a little bit easier. That happened around the 1,500-subscriber mark. It was around this time that I noticed the videos I had been uploading to YouTube were starting to receive comments. People were watching and engaging.

But let me back up. A few months earlier, in March, I had begun a one-year YouTube experiment, the goal being to see how many *active* YouTube subscribers I could generate within twelve months of launching a brand-new channel.

Around this same time, I also noticed that my newly uploaded videos were being watched by the same people. People who had commented on past videos were commenting again and again. It was working, and I thought those commenters must be my subscribers. Awesome, I had a group (a small group but a group nonetheless) of active subscribers: the very thing that the YouTube algorithm rewards.

Statistically, as subscribers view a video, "watch time" metrics improve—the very thing that greatly impacts the placement of a video in both YouTube search and suggested videos. We'll cover both subjects moving forward and more. This is what was happening to my channel around the 3,500-subscriber mark. This resulted in my videos showing up higher in the search results and being recommended as suggested videos. The number of views my videos were getting and the subscriber growth of the channel went through the roof. Considering my channel was just a few months old, these results were outstanding. It was around this time that I realized that I had achieved a new level of growth that could be described as *organic*; this is something that most YouTubers never achieve. Not because they're not talented or skilled. But rather because they didn't take the time to create an overall channel, playlist, and video strategy that acknowledges both viewers as well as the YouTube algorithm.

This book addresses this issue by laying out a battle plan that considers both viewers and the YouTube algorithm.

Weeks later, in October, my channel reached the 4,000-subscriber mark as I headed to Breckenridge, Colorado, for a one-week getaway with my wife. This was to be a working vacation, and my goal was to write a handy little report based on my successful YouTube channel launch and growth up to that point.

As our getaway came to an end, I found that my little report had blossomed to 10,000 words—way too many words for a report, but not enough words for a decent-size book.

I pondered my options, then decided to go forward rather than backward. I decided to take a break from producing and posting videos and spent the entire month of October turning those 10,000 words into a full-blown book.

What you're reading now is the result of that month I spent writing. I called it my *October Book*, you dig? I also took a break in October from updating my YouTube channel with fresh content to illustrate the point that once you reach the aforementioned plateau, YouTube offers momentum and synergy that no other platform can match.

In other words, once you achieve *channel authority*—that is your channel and videos keep viewers watching and coming back for more—YouTube promotes those videos so you get more views and experience subscriber growth seemingly on autopilot.

Great videos can also be evergreen (long-lasting). If you publish a great video on a highly searched for topic, it can rank on YouTube for years and years.

Here's an example: At the time of this writing, if you'd searched YouTube for the phrase "Apple branding," you would have found videos listed in the top twenty results that were two, three, and even ten years old! Ten years! How cool is that? Imagine publishing a video that drove views, gained subscribers, generated leads, and racked up sales for up to ten years.

As October ended, my channel had driven over 55,000 video views and gained over 1,000 new subscribers. With virtually no video uploads during the entire month, that was all autopilot growth, driven by the work I'd done previously. Can you say "residual results"?

However, it wasn't always like that. In fact, at the beginning of my Tube Ritual journey, I published video after video with little to no fanfare. Videos that I spent hours and hours creating, many of which compared to what I'm capable of producing today, were just plain bad.

During this time, I had yet to learn how to publish what I like to refer to as "optimized for YouTube" videos, i.e., videos that drive views and converts viewers into subscribers. This is reality for many YouTubers and entrepreneurs. They beat their creative heads against the wall, and the wall doesn't crack. Why is it that most are unable to upload videos that (a) drive consistent views, and (b) convert viewers into subscribers?

Because, again, most videos are not *optimized for YouTube*, period. YouTubers who use old Google SEO strategies to rank highly on YouTube soon discover that YouTube optimization is less about keywords and much more about viewer engagement and retention. Don't misunderstand. Keyword phrases, metadata, and knowing how to implement them to increase the likelihood that your video will rank is a necessity. However, without *viewer retention*, high-level YouTube success is simply not possible. Keyword phrases and metadata might get you listed somewhere in the search results (like on page seventeen), but they won't get you views or subscribers. That only happens when you focus on creating an engaging experience. Engagement begins with grabbing attention, winning the click, and inspiring viewers to act. Engagement doesn't mean that you need to make people laugh for six minutes straight, do silly pranks, or talk over video games. Engagement is the result of a published video that inspires action. Actions can be in the form of subscribing, sharing, commenting, or simply *watching more and longer*. Note, longer watch time and viewer retention is something YouTube champions, and it's the cornerstone of the YouTube algorithm. This is exactly what this book is about: how to achieve YouTube success by creating an engaging **channel experience** for your audience, understanding how the YouTube algorithm works (what it rewards), and uploading optimized-for-YouTube videos that fuel that fire. The purpose of this book is to share with you seven key pillars of YouTube success. The same seven pillars ultimately allowed me to grow my channel to 5,000 subscribers in roughly six months. Keep in mind that I initially set out on a twelve-month quest to see how big of a channel and subscriber base I could create. This book takes you to the halfway point. I'm only six months in, but my results have been exciting and my actions have resulted in many tips, tactics, and an overall strategy that I will share with you in the pages to come.

THE TUBE RITUAL 30-DAY CHALLENGE

This book provides you with a framework of how to create your own 30-Day Tube Ritual Video Challenge. The goal is to accelerate the growth of your channel. This step is optional and doesn't require daily video uploads.

The key to YouTube success is to regularly publish optimized-for-YouTube videos that engage and keep viewers watching by implementing what I call "The 7 Tube Ritual Success Pillars."

The 7 Tube Ritual Success Pillars

1. How to Stand Out & Get Noticed
2. How to Become Memorable
3. How to Drive More Video Views (Per Viewer)
4. How to Make It Easy for Viewers to Understand Why They Should Subscribe
5. How to Optimize Your Channel for Engagement
6. How to Leverage the Power of Visuals to Entice Viewers to Click
7. How to Create Videos That Keep Viewers Watching Longer

How This Book Is Written

This book is broken up into nine chapters. Early on, we'll focus on branding and building a better mousetrap, one that converts more viewers into subscribers. The Tube Ritual overall strategy is designed to attract a potential viewer's attention, win the click, and deliver an engaging video that inspires viewer engagement (like, comment, share, subscribe, etc.).

You'll learn how to structure your videos to greatly increase the percentage of viewers who end up taking the action you want them to take. We'll also cover playlist strategies that will lead to more views, which will help your videos rank higher in search results and appear in YouTube's suggested video recommendations.

Later, in Chapter Nine, we'll cover the step-by-step specifics of uploading videos to YouTube, including tips on how to optimize your videos to appeal to the YouTube algorithm. Even better, I'll hook you up with *free software* that will integrate the Tube Ritual upload checklist right into the YouTube upload dashboard.

Free YouTube Software

Rank your videos and drive more views by integrating the Tube Ritual 12-Step Upload Checklist right into your YouTube dashboard. To get your free checklist go to: ***BrianGJohnson.TV/Free***

CHAPTER ONE

Numbers Don't Lie

Rule number one: YouTube doesn't pick channel winners or losers. Yes, the algorithm determines which videos will be heavily promoted across the YouTube website; however, those results are driven by the *actions* (or lack thereof) *of viewers*. It's the viewers who ultimately determine the success or failure of videos on YouTube. YouTube simply displays the results.

I've said it before and I'll say it again and again and again, **engagement is king**. I've heard YouTubers complain that YouTube must hate them because their videos tank. They go on and on about using keywords, optimizing tags, titles, descriptions, creating great thumbnails and more, generally adhering to YouTube's best practices. But, if viewers don't like, and thus watch, their videos (again, watching is a form of engagement) all the tweaking in the world won't help. Viewers hold all the cards, so that is what we'll focus on moving forward.

Publish engaging videos and viewers will:

• Watch more of your videos

- Watch your videos for longer periods of time
- Subscribe to your channel
- Like your videos
- Share your videos
- Comment on videos

You also want viewers to become loyalists, so they will help build your brand, buy your products or services, visit your website, and put money in your pocket.

You'll learn how YouTube helps you achieve those goals by rewarding you for creating content that garners more views and longer watch times.

I know this may sound like a daunting task, but the tips and strategies described in this book—the very tips and strategies that I use every day—will pave the way for your success.

Early on, before you have a subscriber base, you must be able to attract views via YouTube search and suggested videos. For example, if you don't target not only keywords but the right kind of keywords, **relevant keywords**, you'll struggle to grow your channel. Video titles, tags and descriptions, also known as metadata, are critically important. Setting these fields up correctly when you upload a video helps YouTube identify the content and target the search results your video should potentially show up in. I say potentially because if the video isn't engaging, it may never show up at all.

Expedite Your Growth with Just One More Video

Much of this book focuses on two elements: YouTube SEO (search engine optimization) and increasing engagement. However, the last chapter, Chapter Nine, will encourage you to create your own personal thirty-day video challenge. Again, this is an optional step you may want to integrate into your action plan as you move forward.

I set the challenge at thirty days because I believe that's what brings maximum results in the shortest amount of time; but if that's too daunting, set your own parameters. Maybe you can publish one engaging video every other day, or once weekly. Again, this is a goal you can set yourself. The key is to publish engaging videos consistently and often.

Remember this formula:

Engaging content x frequency x relevancy = views

Note, subscriber growth is directly tied to the number of video views your channel receives. As you drive more views, you'll gain more subscribers. Thus, focus on these three factors and you'll expedite your results. As shown in the image below, I saw a growth in views of 439 percent in 43 days, going from 300 to 1,200-plus views daily on a channel that was just days old.

I shared a very early and nonoptimized version of this exact "Ritual Challenge" method with YouTuber Dan Brock, and he too saw his channel explode with game-changing results.

The goal is simple: Publish as many YouTube-optimized videos as possible within a specified period. Thirty days is a great starting point, but if you're hungry for results, shoot for a video a day for as long as you can.

I challenged myself to a sixty-day challenge and ran out of steam around day fifty, and while I did not reach my goal, my channel still blew up.

Dan Brock experienced similar results by focusing on "just one more video" day after day, and the results were amazing. His channel grew by 400 percent, from 600 to 2,400 subscribers, as a direct result of his efforts. By the way, Dan posted daily videos for approximately a 30-day period. He'll tell you the result was worth the effort. Today Dan has over 20,000 subscribers. Amazing.

Why is participating in a challenge like this so powerful, and why does it work so well? In short, once you've accepted a challenge, you're focused on the *process of producing and uploading optimized-for-YouTube videos*. This allows you to target far more keyword phrases and thus, you increase your overall channel views. You'll also be forced to hone your production and editing skills and improve your on-camera presence and all the other things that go into creating engaging videos.

A Tube Ritual Challenge is different than most other YouTube challenges because not only are you uploading lots of videos, you're doing it in a manner that is strategically designed to drive more views and increase viewer engagement. These things, from research to production to final upload, play a part in how viewers perceive your videos and thus how the algorithm ranks your videos. They also help convert viewers who discover your channel for the first time into subscribers.

Keep in mind that frequency and consistency drive results, but you can take part in a challenge as much or as little as you want. Implement the Ritual strategies and tactics found in this book and your channel will grow. Add a thirty-day challenge to the mix and you'll expedite that growth just like Dan and I did. Now it's your turn.

My Own, Far Bigger "Tube Ritual" Challenge

On March 1, 2016, I launched a brand-new YouTube Channel, **Brian G Johnson TV**, with the goal of gaining 25,000 subscribers within one year. It was a lofty goal, considering that I wasn't targeting a niche with a massive viewer base such as gaming, beauty, or tech. Rather, my channel would focus on online marketing, specifically, how to *amplify your message* and *inspire action* with the use of video.

Today, Thursday, December 8, 2016, as I write this, it's month nine of my Tube Ritual case study. Just days ago, I reached 6,440 subscribers. While I am way off my target of 25,000 subscribers, I am on track to hit 10,000 subscribers in a one-year period. To put my progress into perspective, consider this: one of the most successful channels in my niche recently surpassed the 250,000-subscriber mark. At its one-year anniversary, this same channel had approximately 10,000 subscribers. Over the last few months, as my videos have gotten more and more views, my subscriber base has grown at a tremendous rate. My focus has been to drive more views with each new video upload and to convert viewers into subscribers.

249 Percent Increase in Subscribers July 4 – Oct 1

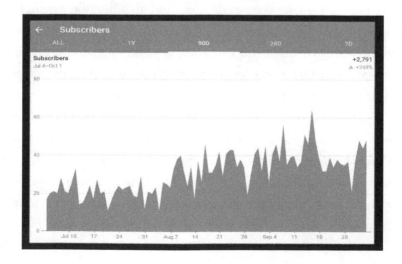

Do the same, and you'll win. I'll also mention here that my views-to-subscriber ratio, that is the percentage of viewers who act and subscribe, is well above average at 1.97 percent. For example, for each 1,000 YouTube views my channel drives, nineteen of those viewers click to become subscribers.

I recently crunched the numbers of some of the top YouTube marketing video creators to gauge just how well I was converting viewers into subscribers compared to them. What I found was that the views-to-subscriber ratio varied quite a bit, from 0.6 percent to 2.4 percent. My channel came in second highest at 1.97 percent. So, for every 1,000 video views, these channels gained between 6 and 24 subscribers.

The moral of the story is this: if you want to drive more views, gain more subscribers, build a list, or make money on YouTube, read this book and put the strategies into play. It really is as simple as that. This is great progress, but remember, those exciting stats and all those views, subscribers, and overall channel growth would not have happened if I had not implemented the strategies within this book.

My growth began in June 2016, three months *after* I had launched my new channel. At the time, my YouTube growth would have made you yawn. I drove a few views here and there, and my subscriber rate in May was an average of four to eight daily. I'll be honest, my first three months were incredibly challenging. I had a hard time ranking videos, my views were not increasing, and I began to wonder what I had gotten myself into. However, by this time I had created what I call my "duplicatable video creation system." A duplicatable video creation system is just that: *a system that makes it possible to easily and often create optimized-for-YouTube videos.* You dig? Good! Because it's super-important. This is why you see so many YouTubers whose backgrounds are nearly, if not always, the same. They leverage the power of a set (also known as a video backdrop) and a system. They rely on their set in order to move forward and create optimized-for-YouTube videos often. Deviating from their set would take time, energy, and sometimes money—time and energy that could have been used to create and publish more videos. During those first few frustrating months, I was all over the place and I was far from being able to create optimized videos regularly. However, I was giving myself time to learn new skills—the skills needed to create my duplicatable *video creation system*. I was learning video lighting, a DSLR camera, video editing, how to craft eye-catching thumbnails, and more. The question becomes this:

At this point in your journey, have you created your very own duplicatable video creation system—one that makes it easier for you to regularly create and upload optimized-for-YouTube videos?

If not, are you in the YouTuber learning stage, i.e., you're learning to operate a camera, use editing software, and improve the lighting of your videos? Fantastic, the process can be challenging but it's also incredibly rewarding. Be willing to publish videos as you learn, and you'll be able to see your own YouTube growth. If you are in the learning stages, I suggest you keep things simple. You do not need fancy graphics, effects, jump cuts, an expensive camera, or expensive editing software to succeed on YouTube.

Sure, I use all these things today, however, I've spent the last ten years practicing the craft and I've also worked on improving my *video creation system* and I was willing to invest both money and time to improve the overall quality of my videos. However, it's not necessary to spend a ton of money on equipment when you're first starting out.

You can create great videos today with just your mobile phone. In fact, one of my most successful videos was created using my iPhone. This video has terrible lighting and bad audio, but it drives thousands of views each month and gains my channel subscribers. That would not have happened if I was not willing to publish less than perfect videos during my learning stages. There are YouTubers with tens of thousands of subscribers who use an iPhone and natural light to record, edit, and upload videos. I've also seen YouTubers with millions of subscribers use nothing more than simple whiteboard animation videos.

What's important is **creating engaging content**, not the method through which the content was created. Engaging content can be created with the simplest of tools.

There are YouTubers generating millions of views with videos recorded on their iPhones. In turn, there are YouTubers getting zero views, and they're using a $2,000 camera. Start where you are, use what you have, and most importantly, begin at once. Don't complicate matters with expensive equipment and complex software. YouTube rewards engagement, not $2,000 cameras.

CHAPTER TWO

Your Goal & Plan of Action

I f you want to get more views and subscribers, make a commitment to yourself right now to focus on the process of creating great videos. If you're in the learning stages, then know this: Publish more videos, and they'll get better. It'll happen on its own simply by publishing more. Even better, the quality improvement of your videos will greatly impact your ability to convert viewers into subscribers. Yes, quality matters, but it's not everything, so don't go overboard with overanalyzing quality. Sometimes you need to know when enough is enough. However, improving the quality of your videos is a good thing, so keep improving over time.

The Goal

To clarify, the goal is to **create channel growth quickly**, not publish a video for thirty days straight on YouTube. Heck, you can upload daily, every other day, or twice a week. The point is to set a challenging goal and go for it. Create a production schedule, and stick to it.

I'm getting ready to do another challenge, and I'm pumped because I've seen the results time and again of previous challenges. Also, keep in mind that once you have completed the initial challenge, you do not have to continue to publish at such a high rate to see continued growth in views and subscribers. If your videos are engaging and have high watch time, YouTube growth will happen. Admittedly, it's hard to gain momentum and authority on YouTube. Once you have it, however, it's easy to maintain by publishing a weekly video or more if you're so inclined. As mentioned earlier, I took off the entire month of October and watched from the sidelines as my videos continued to drive results day after day. A **Tube Ritual Challenge** makes it possible to gain that momentum and authority quickly. I did it, and you too can do it. Note, if you are not able to commit to thirty days, no problem. Instead, push for twenty days or ten. Whatever you're able to do and move forward with, do that. Take the next step committing to a Tube Ritual Challenge yourself. Mark up your calendar, online scheduler, or whatever you need to do to make it happen.

CHAPTER THREE

Playlist & Thumbnail Ritual

Phase One

Chances are if you've spent any amount of time researching the topic of how to grow a successful channel, you've run into countless videos, blog posts, podcasts and more. There are many genuine, knowledgeable YouTube experts whose advice can help you grow your channel.

However, there are far more so-called experts pedaling quick fixes, hacks, and software that promise results, most of which simply don't work. That leaves us with one important question: How do you know what's important and what to focus on when it comes to driving results?

Fortunately, a post on the YouTube Creator Blog tells us **exactly** what matters most. In a word: **engagement**.

YouTube Creator Blog

YouTube search, now optimized for time watched
Friday, October 12, 2012

"We've started adjusting the ranking
of videos in YouTube search to reward
engaging videos that
keep viewers watching."

When it comes to achieving high-level YouTube success, nothing is more important than publishing engaging videos. Or as YouTube puts it, "engaging videos that keep viewers watching." Do that extremely well and you can make numerous "mistakes" and it will not matter. You'll be wildly successful, just ask Casey Neistat, one of the most successful YouTubers of late. Of course, that's not all that matters, but it's a huge piece of the puzzle. YouTube says so itself, which makes it easier to **prioritize** what's most important.

At the time of this writing, I've published 150-plus videos to my channel, so I have a pretty good basis of comparison and plenty of statistics to show what works and what doesn't. My YouTube statistics show that my most engaging videos (those that keep viewers watching longer) drive more views via YouTube search and Suggested Videos than my videos that viewers find less engaging.

This is simply because YouTube considers my most engaging videos worthy of being promoted across their site because they are *"engaging videos that keep viewers watching"* just like the blog post said.

One question I'm often asked is, how long does one need to keep viewers watching to gain authority with YouTube? This question is hard to answer, but in my opinion the one thing you don't want to do is string viewers along. By that I mean artificially lengthening a video with the hopes of improving rankings. Because subscribers are so critically important to YouTube channel growth, you want to take care of their needs first. Most of the time, viewers want the information as quickly as possible. Thus, I do my best to create the shortest videos possible without sacrificing video content.

That means not cutting out any critical elements needed to teach, make someone laugh, and/or both. For example, one of my first high-ranking videos covers mobile editing with iMovie. The video is around twenty minutes long, and I cover a lot of helpful information. Most viewers really like the video. It's funny and goes into depth. Today, I might have been able to "cut" a minute or two from the video, reducing the length from twenty minutes to eighteen. Thus, as you move forward, the goal should not be to make short videos, but rather to cut as much as possible from the videos you make. If you feel a section is dragging on, cut it. The sooner you deliver value, the more likely you'll retain more viewers and thus achieve higher rankings.

My goal is to simply create engaging videos that viewers enjoy and deem valuable. By doing that, everybody wins. Value comes in many shapes and sizes and lengths on YouTube. If you teach something to someone, there's a good chance they will find your video valuable. If you make someone laugh, or brighten their day, even better.

Let's talk about the power of "different" for a moment.

When I set out on my year-long Tube Ritual journey, my goal was to create videos that were fun and different from anything already on YouTube. Different, by nature, can be engaging. There are lots of people who address the same topic as I do on YouTube, but they are not me. We are all different (in an awesome way!!). If you know me, or if you've watched any of my videos, you know that my style is different from most YouTubers who teach marketing. And some people are not fans. They think I'm hokey or goofy, but that's okay because my statistics show that those who do like my style and message are engaged and responding in a big way.

I knew going in that not everybody would dig what I was doing or even like me, and that was okay. However, that does not mean that a negative comment does not hurt. It can and often does; however, I am not willing to bend on who I am and what's important to me. I learned years ago that if you try to please everyone, in the end, you end up pleasing no one, not even yourself.

So, my advice is this: If you are just starting out, make videos that you'd like to watch, videos that make *you* happy. You'll do your best work and chances are, you'll build an audience that appreciates you for you. Let's get back to the previous question: How long does one need to keep viewers watching before YouTube considers a video to be of adequate watch time and deserve promotion?

In your YouTube dashboard, you'll find a metric that gauges "audience retention" (how long viewers watch). You'll also find "relative audience retention," which measures how engaging a video is compared to other YouTube videos.

YouTube Help explains how to read the graph you find there. "When the graph is higher, it indicates how many more viewers kept watching your video for that timeframe compared to the same timeframe in other YouTube videos."

Combine that with the previously mentioned post from the YouTube Creator Blog regarding YouTube's emphasis on engagement, and you get this framework to chart your results:

Create videos that viewers find engaging and watch longer, then track your progress via YouTube Analytics and "relative audience retention" (RAR).

The YouTube algorithm is highly complex and considers many factors. However, by keeping the process simple, you can focus on what matters most to not only viewers but to YouTube as well.

I've also noticed a correlation between my best ranking videos and an above-average RAR score. The higher the score, the faster YouTube seems to promote that video via search and Suggested Videos.

One of my more recent videos had an incredibly high RAR score, and on the third day, YouTube began promoting the video in YouTube search.

Check out the following graphs to see how I charted this video's progress and traffic sources.

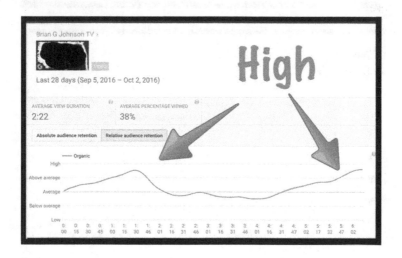

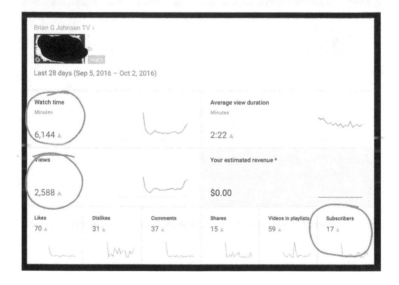

Traffic source	Watch time (minutes) ↓	Views
YouTube search	2,960 (48%)	1,327 (51%)
Suggested videos	1,267 (21%)	561 (22%)
Browse features	695 (11%)	209 (8.1%)
Direct or unknown	514 (8.4%)	181 (7.0%)
External	304 (5.0%)	129 (5.0%)
YouTube channels	198 (3.2%)	65 (2.5%)
Notifications	83 (1.4%)	42 (1.6%)
Other YouTube features	56 (0.9%)	37 (1.4%)
End screens	34 (0.5%)	22 (0.9%)
Playlists	22 (0.4%)	10 (0.4%)
Playlist page	11 (0.2%)	5 (0.2%)

Brian G Johnson TV ›

Last 28 days (Sep 5, 2016 – Oct 2, 2016)

Watch time	Average view duration
Minutes	Minutes
6,144	2:22

Views	Your estimated revenue *
2,588	$0.00

Likes	Dislikes	Comments	Shares	Videos in playlists	Subscribers
70	31	37	15	59	17

Analytics & The Elements

YouTube provides a tremendous amount of data and I am constantly studying these metrics to improve my video and channel performance. I also focus my attention on other elements including views, subscribers, and more that ultimately drive success on YouTube.

To access your YouTube analytics, log in to your YouTube account, click "Video Manager" at the top menu, then click "ANALYTICS" in the left menu.

Video & Channel Engagement

I'm going to say it again. The most important thing to remember about building your YouTube channel is this:

> *YouTube actively promotes channels and videos that viewers engage with. Watching more is a form of engagement.*

Write that down. Commit it to memory. Print it on a T-shirt. Do whatever you must to keep that thought at the forefront of your YouTube brain. It really is that important.

YouTube doesn't arbitrarily decide which channels will succeed and which channels will not. YouTube gives authority to those videos and channels that viewers like, watch, and engage with. That's it.

Channels that keep viewers coming back and watching longer are of critical importance to YouTube. YouTube gives authority to videos that have proven their worth by getting lots of views and garnering longer watch times.

YouTube makes money selling advertising inventory. So, while YouTube talks about "rewarding engaging videos," understand that they also reward engaging channels. Channels, not individual videos, are what draws viewers back to YouTube. If you like one video in a channel, chances are you'll like them all or at least check them out.

Channels provide the "stickiness" that has driven YouTube to not only become the largest and most-heavily-trafficked video site on the web but the third most popular website overall.

That's why the goal of a Tube Ritual Challenge is not only to publish a lot of videos over a thirty-day period but to **create an engaging channel**

experience that keeps viewers clicking, watching, and returning. Do that, and you'll win.

Where Are All Those Views Coming From?

If a video is driving an above-average number of views for my channel, then I want to know *why is that video getting so many views?* Is the video featured high in search or being featured in Suggested Videos? Is the video converting viewers into subscribers and are viewers engaging with the video? What is the relative audience retention (RAR) of the video?

All these factors can and do contribute to YouTube success. Understanding these details will help you make better decisions as you publish future videos.

Active Subscribers Drive Momentum & Success

As a YouTube channel gains *active* subscribers, it becomes *slightly* easier to drive more views, increase relative audience retention, and in turn, gain even more subscribers. A channel gains momentum based on the fundamentals of how the YouTube algorithm works. These fundamentals include:

- View Velocity
- Accumulated Watch Time
- Audience Retention

View velocity refers to how many views a video receives within the first twenty-four to seventy-two hours of release. The more views the better because the algorithm keeps up with such things and gives priority to videos with high view velocity. Many YouTube experts believe that the algorithm looks at how many views a new video drives compared to the size of the subscriber base.

For example, if you have 100 subscribers and a new video drives fifty views in the first twenty-four hours, that's a very high view velocity and YouTube may reward you for it by promoting that video to a broader audience. Thus, as a channel gains more active subscribers, the view velocity increases to each newly published video, adding subscribers for the win.

It gets better. My statistics show that subscribers watch my videos around 30 percent longer than nonsubscribers. That's why you want viewers to subscribe—because subscribers watch longer, the very thing that YouTube rewards. For example, if I publish a ten-minute video, the video's average view duration for nonsubscribers may be three minutes; meaning that, on average, nonsubscribers watch for three minutes before moving along. However, the average view duration for subscribers may be four minutes. As a channel gains more and more **ACTIVE** subscribers, video *watch time metrics* become stronger with more views, longer view durations, a higher relative audience retention score, and more accumulated watch time.

What Is Watch Time?

This brings us to our next metric, the biggie, the one everyone talks about: **watch time**. YouTube often mentions watch time when referring to all these metrics together:

- Audience Retention
- Average View Duration
- Watch Time
- Average Percentage Viewed

This makes things a bit more complicated. Watch time is its own metric and used to address all metrics that gauge "how long viewers are watching."

"Accumulated watch time" is like the fuel that allows a video to rank for a given keyword phrase. For example, if you want to rank highly for a popular term like "lose weight," you may need one million minutes of watch time. This is the *accumulated* amount of time that viewers have watched your video. Statistically speaking, as my videos have gained more Accumulated watch time, discoverability has improved and views have increased.

SIDE NOTE: I've mentioned "discoverability" several times now. This simply means a video is discoverable in YouTube search and Suggested Videos, two of the biggest sources of traffic on YouTube. We'll talk lots more about both search and Suggested Videos in the coming pages.

This is why subscribers have such a big impact on channel growth. And for the sake of clarity going forward, when I use the term "subscriber," I'll be referring to ACTIVE subscribers, i.e., those subscribers who interact with your channel regularly, rather than those who might have subscribed but never watched a single minute of your videos.

There are many hacks and cheats that make it easy to get subscribers. You can bribe viewers into subscribing. You can entice them with giveaways and rewards. You can even buy subscribers, but unless they're ACTIVE, you'll just be compiling numbers that mean nothing, i.e., numbers that will not drive real growth or leads or sales.

Make no mistake, nonactive subscribers DO NOT help channels grow and may even put a channel at a disadvantage. Keep in mind, some experts believe that YouTube measures Video Views and the percentage of subscribers who are viewing. Thus, if a channel has 10,000 nonactive subscribers that never log watch time, the percentage of subscribers who are watching new videos as they're released will statistically be much lower than what YouTube considers an average.

This brings me to what I personally look for when studying my analytics and video views. I would rather publish a video that drives ten views a day and gains four subscribers than a video that drives one hundred views and gains just two subscribers.

Active subscribers who watch and engage are the juice that powers successful channels!

My Simple Formula for YouTube Success

Here's the simple formula I use to measure YouTube success. Remember, RAR is relative audience retention.

Above Average RAR + Keyword Relevancy + SEO = More Views

To look at a video's RAR, log in to your YouTube Creator Studio account and do the following:

1. Select Video Manager
2. Select the video you want to measure
3. Select Analytics Button
4. Select Average View Duration
5. Select Relative Audience Retention

Engagement Ritual

Fortunately, you can formulate the process of creating engaging videos. As I studied the outer and inner workings of YouTube and watched videos from other leading experts such as Tim Schmoyer and

Derral Eves, I heard them often mention the importance of studying YouTube analytics, especially Audience Retention, and to repeat what worked.

When I first heard this advice, I wondered how I could duplicate the retention metrics of a video. It was then I started to realize how powerful it is to try different things, especially in the first sixty seconds of a video (the intro). The lesson I learned was that the intro can make or break a video's success.

If you don't engage the viewer quickly and hold their attention, video retention will suffer as will potential rankings. With this knowledge in hand, I came up with various intros and began testing. These included the mad scientist intro as well as the cowhand, both of which are characters that I add into my videos, which my audience responds to (in a positive way).

I also leveraged time-tested sales copy phrases such as:

- Imagine
- If/Then

In the "imagine" intro, I simply prompted the viewer to imagine the thing they were after. "Imagine being able to rank videos and drive more views." The "if and then" sales copy hook is simple and has been handed down from marketer to marketer over the years, originating from Gary Halbert. You simply begin your email, sales letter, or video with: *If you want to _____ (fill in the blank), then you won't want to miss a single second of this video, and here's why.*

After I began experimenting, I could identify what type of intros worked and which ones did not. I wondered what would happen if I repeated a video intro that had worked well in the past. Sure enough, what worked once, worked twice . . . heck, it even worked three times.

So, as you move forward, understand there's no reason why you can't repeat various styles, intros, music, editing techniques, and more.

Be willing to try different things, knowing that by experimenting you'll get different engagement levels. On the other hand, if you always create nearly the same type of videos, you may be stuck with that level of engagement.

Video Engagement Scale

When it comes to engagement, not all videos are created equally. Videos that contain a person speaking directly into the camera are generally more engaging than videos that don't have a person in them.

For example, consider two videos that each cover the same topic, say how to install an app.

Most people would rather watch a video that has a person walking (and talking) them through the process than a video that doesn't have a face connected to a voice.

I personally hate videos that lack any form of human element. You've seen them, those videos with annoying music beats, but no on-camera host or voiceover. Humans relate to other humans. It's far easier to hold a viewer's attention if you're in the video in some shape, form, or fashion.

Not everyone is comfortable in front of a camera. If you don't want to put yourself in the video that's cool, but I would encourage you to do a voiceover rather than rely on stock music or other tactics viewers may find less engaging and more annoying. Lending your voice to the video will allow you to tell an engaging story, guide viewers along, and use the thing that is naturally engaging: your own voice.

One thing I hear a lot is, "I have a face for radio." Unfortunately, most people do not have a VOICE for radio, but neither of those things ultimately matter.

"Engaging" doesn't mean that you must look like Angelina Jolie or sound like Barry White. In fact, most successful YouTubers are not "beautiful people." Many present an image or persona that is "different," and different can be even more engaging than beautiful. If being on-camera or narrating a video frightens you, I encourage you to push through and try, because doing so is the path to creating more engaging videos.

CHAPTER FOUR

Win the Click

Be Memorable & Make a Statement

If you want to grow a successful YouTube channel, you must accomplish these three goals:

1. Grab the viewer's attention and make a statement
2. Win the click
3. Convert more viewers into subscribers

Grabbing Attention & Winning the Click

"Winning the click" is the phrase that video marketing expert **Owen Hemsath** coined in a video we collaborated on. The subject matter of that video was how anyone can get more clicks and thus video views. Owen recommended "winning the click" by working smart.

The process begins by demanding the viewer's attention. That part is easy, once you have the knowledge that I'm about to share. To illustrate how this works, you need to put yourself in the place of a YouTube viewer and realize how most viewers browse YouTube.

In its most basic sense, YouTube is a platform for serving up videos over the web. At the heart of that platform is the web's second most popular search engine (after Google).

The typical YouTube experience begins with the viewer entering keywords to search for or clicking thumbnails featured on their YouTube homepage.

On YouTube, the viewer always has lots of click options, whether they're searching for specific keywords or actively watching a video. YouTube offers viewers a variety of click options in a variety of ways.

Did you get that? Let me say it again: YouTube provides search results based on the browsing habits and most recent searches the viewer has done. This is known as viewer history. As a result, the viewer is presented with a plethora of options, all from different channels.

In the example image shown next, I searched for "how to edit videos." You can see the variety of click options YouTube presented to me.

In the above screen capture, Derral Eves's thumbnail is clearly winning visually. The thumbnail makes great use of contrast, the white and yellow text stands out against the black background, and his face is front and center. You can't win the click unless the viewer is visually drawn to your thumbnail and thereby, enticed to click. YouTube is a visual medium. Viewers use their eyes first to decide which videos to watch. If your thumbnail lacks appeal, as most in that screenshot do, chances are your views will suffer. Thumbnails aside, keep in mind that what we're looking at are **different results** from **different channels** and nothing stands out.

However, by working smart, we can stand out by:

- Targeting search terms that are easier to rank for
- Creating thumbnails based on themes
- Leveraging congruent colors, fonts, and style
- Driving more views from one search query

For example, in the following screenshot of an actual YouTube search result, my thumbnails make a statement because I followed two simple but powerful rules. These rules lead to tremendous results as you'll soon discover.

1. I targeted a less competitive term(s).
2. My thumbnails are based on a playlist template.

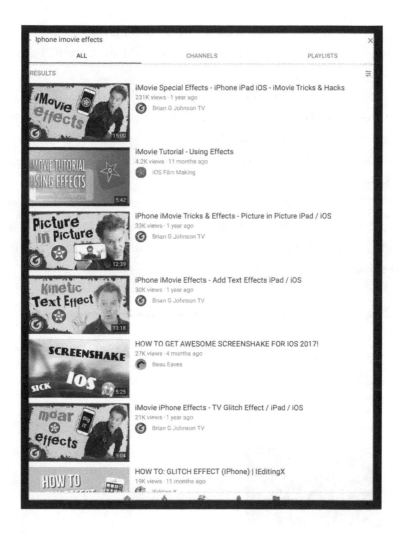

The result is a congruency in color, style, and brand. Furthermore, the multiple thumbnails let viewers know that I cover this subject in-depth because I have so many videos on the topic. I am much more likely to win the click.

Again, keep in mind that it's not just the number of views a YouTube channel gets that dictates success. How viewers interact with your content and engage with your channel come into play as well.

For example, someone searching for "iPhone iMovie" or similar search terms is likely to watch *several* of my videos on related topics, rather than just one.

This sends a **MASSIVE ENGAGEMENT SIGNAL** to YouTube that viewers REALLY like my *channel*. Knowing that engagement is fuel to the algorithm fire means that YouTube is far more likely to reward my channel in the future by exposing my videos via high search results and in Suggested Videos.

As I am writing this book, I've started to notice that more and more people are now searching YouTube for my name plus topics that relate to my channel. Bingo! That means I've created an engaging channel experience, one that's memorable and keeps viewers coming back.

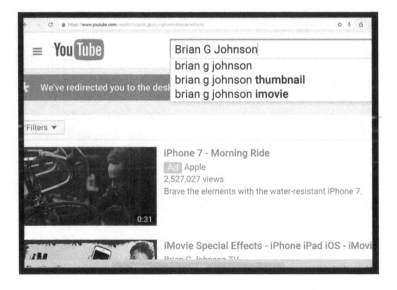

Notice in the screenshot that these two topics (iMovie and thumbnails) are related. They both fall under YouTube video creation. Do you think someone who is interested in learning about iMovie would also be interested in learning how to design a thumbnail? I think so.

We'll talk more about the importance and power of related topics in the coming pages. For now, let's continue to examine how you can easily grab attention and win that click!

Let's talk about consistency of brand and congruent design for a moment. In the above screen capture, notice that all the thumbnails contain my brand logo in the lower left corner, which is always yellow.

Every one of my thumbnails also has my signature "splat" borders. They all use similar fonts and incorporate my brand style. All modesty aside, my thumbnails are eye-catching, engaging, and drive viewers to click.

Also, note that by targeting specific keyword themes in your niche and going deep (producing many videos on a given subject) you have the chance to show up multiple times in the search results, as well as in Suggested Videos.

When viewers see lots of engaging thumbnails that obviously belong to the same channel, it gives that channel authority in the viewer's eyes. Perception is reality! Look at those cool thumbnails from that channel. They shout from the rooftops! Surely, this guy must know his stuff! Let's click to find out!

The YouTube Playlist & Thumbnail Ritual-Phase One

Thumbnails are also extremely important when it comes to branding playlists within your YouTube channel. Check out this screenshot of two playlists from my channel and notice the obvious similarities and differences.

My overall thumbnail design is consistent, but I use different background colors to visually differentiate thumbnails from different playlists—tan background for "iPhone iMovie Tutorial Videos" and the yellow background for "Apps for Editing Videos."

Some elements are the same across all my playlists.

All the thumbnails in the first playlist include:

- Brand logo (YouTube profile picture)
- Brand logo placement (lower left corner)
- Brand logo color (yellow & black)
- iMovie icon
- Exact same background color (tan)

- Same font
- Same border
- Color: pop of red
- Picture of me (features my face)

The common traits are shared among the thumbnails in the second playlist. The only difference is the color of the background and text.

We'll dive deeper into the art and science of creating a well performing YouTube playlist shortly. For now, understand that the goal is to come up with brand assets (imagery) that you can leverage in your YouTube channel art, profile picture and thumbnails.

The Result of Congruent Design

The human eye is drawn to repeating patterns and themes. This is exactly why I created my thumbnails (after a lot of testing and research) in this manner. What happened when I implemented these rules of congruent design across all my thumbnails? Viewers began to binge watch my videos. Time and again, I have read comments from viewers like, "just watched a bunch of your videos."

A bonus of getting comments like this is that such viewer activity signals the algorithm with each click. Hey, this channel is engaging and viewers tend to watch multiple videos. Which of course, adds more watch time, increases audience retention, and results in more subscribers. That click was won!

This is the type of channel experience you want to create. I'm proud of my brand. It's different, it's fun, and it's memorable. You too can create a memorable channel experience by creating a congruent and harmonious brand.

Create Congruency in Your Brand

You create a congruent brand by using the same or similar:

- Brand colors
- Brand fonts
- Brand style
- Content themes
- Sound bites
- Editing style
- And more . . .

A brand is not so much about what color you select for your logo, but rather how you want to *make people feel* and the message you want to convey.

Thus, colors, fonts, music, sound effects, style, and more are selected based on your message and how you want people to feel when they land on your channel page or website and when they watch a video or listen to you on a podcast.

Consistency of branding is key to YouTube success.

What's Your Brand Message?

My brand message is simple: Brian G Johnson is fun, silly, unabashedly himself, and shares the very strategies and tactics he uses to **inspire action in others**: the very thing that's needed for **success**. He does this by **staking his claim** and **amplifying his message**, and he can teach you to do the same. How simple is that?

We'll talk more about crafting your message in an upcoming section, which deals with making it easy for people to understand why your channel is worthy of them subscribing. Read on!

Channel Building Blocks: Pieces of a Puzzle That Together Become One

As YouTube creators, we have access to many assets that allow us to make a statement. In the previous example, I shared how my thumbnails are not singular units, but rather, parts of a puzzle that fit together as one, and together my thumbnails make a statement.

That statement is, *this channel is worth exploring.*

As you build your channel by creating playlists, uploading videos, adding channel art, and more, ask yourself, how is this singular element going to fit into my overall channel theme?

How will these colors work for this playlist?

How will my profile picture look next to my channel art?

My channel art includes my signature splats, color palette, and style. It fits well with my profile picture and thumbnails. It works on its own and together and represents a well thought-out brand.

Alone, all the building blocks that make up my channel are strong, however, together they are far more powerful. Why? Because I repeat the same type of fonts, colors, style, and logo. As humans, we're far more likely to remember something if we hear, see, and experience it again and again and again.

YouTube Channel Assets (Building Blocks)

Here is how I'm leveraging the following channel assets.

Profile Picture

The profile picture is the small, round icon that shows up at the top of your channel. Most YouTubers use an image of their face. Incorporating your face in your channel art and or video thumbnails is recommended. Studies show that images with faces are more powerful when it comes to building trust and driving results via social media.

YouTube has stated that thumbnails that incorporate a face **statistically drive more clicks**, so I usually include my face in my thumbnails. I also include a picture of me in my channel art. However, for the profile picture I use my logo for the following reasons.

First of all, the profile picture is very small and it's hard to see a face, but my logo stands out. Because it is small, I can also add my logo to each of my thumbnails. The result is congruency. No matter what, each of my thumbnails is always going to contain my logo, in the same color, and usually in the same position (lower lefthand corner).

Furthermore, my video intro, which is short at just under five seconds, contains my logo, as does my website and my social media graphics.

My logo acts as my reminder to say, "Hey! It's me, Brian G.!" This is something I say at the beginning of my videos (spoken congruency). The point I'm making is that repetition is a powerful thing.

Notice, in the above image, each thumbnail contains my logo in the lower lefthand corner. As you move forward with your channel (and brand) you may want to use a logo for your profile picture and incorporate your logo into your video thumbnails.

SIDE NOTE: The YouTube profile picture shows up every time you comment on a video and shows up against a white background. So, you may want to choose a color palette that pops against white. That's why I use the black and white version of my logo for my profile picture.

YouTube Channel Art

Also known as the *channel header*, YouTube channel art is the large graphic that is placed at the top of every YouTube channel. Designing your YouTube channel art is a bit tricky in that it must be sized for mobile devices including phones and tablets, as well as televisions and computers. However, there is a channel art template that makes the process easier and provides guides when it comes to where to incorporate images, text, and so on. If you're not a graphic designer, I suggest you hire a professional to create your channel art for you. Your channel art plays a big role when it comes to converting viewers into subscribers. If your channel art is subpar, that will affect your subscriber growth in a negative manner. Get the best design you can and keep the brand congruent across all elements.

YouTube graphic assets include:

- Channel art
- Profile picture
- Thumbnail templates

Channel Art Resources, Options & Examples

Great channel art doesn't have to cost an arm and a leg. You can get the job done very inexpensively (Fiverr.com), or you can hire a designer that you like and have worked with in the past. Earlier, I mentioned Nick Nimmin. Nick is a graphics whiz who offers professional graphic packages that are also fairly priced. Check out Nick's Tuber Tools website for more details. The URL is TuberTools.com

For example, when I hired Matt at *TweetPages.com*, I knew the feel and experience I wanted to convey. I knew I wanted a bold, in your face, rock 'n' roll Western or branded look. We spoke at length about this. I shared various images and ideas that gave Matt a baseline to start with, and the result was AWESOME!

When it comes to YouTube channel art, I am a big believer in less is more. Apple's branding and imagery embody this simple principle. Channel art should incorporate a picture of you or an image that represents the type of video content you create, not a ton of images and hard to read text.

Simple is better, less is more. I highly suggest that you use an image of yourself because people gravitate toward those they know, like, and trust. This is especially true if you're in the marketing space and/or you're using your channel in a business-related way.

Just for fun, try this experiment: Real fast, without thinking, grab a pen and a piece of paper. Now (again fast) write the names of some of your favorite YouTubers. Next, check their channels and see how many of them use their face in their channel art. Understand that there are no hard and fast rules here. The exception might be video gaming channels, where the focus is more on the games rather than the YouTuber recording the videos.

Check out this twelve-year-old boy with over a million subscribers. He gets it. There's a photo of him, brand colors, same font, less is more. Bingo.

The Ritual Thumbnail Playlist *Style* Strategy

As mentioned before, do not think of thumbnails on a singular basis. That is, do not create individual thumbnails with totally different designs for each individual video you create. Rather, focus on creating a thumbnail style that will be applied to all videos within the playlists. You can create a thumbnail style by repeating the use of a font, or font style, font color, images, graphics or logos, and so on.

Notice these two playlists each have a "thumbnail theme." They both incorporate a white background; however, the thumbnail playlist is a tan color.

AUTHOR'S NOTE: This book was written in October 2016. This note was added in February 2017. Over that time, I updated and tweaked my thumbnails. I wanted to mention this for several reasons. First, YouTube is a journey and an art, and art takes time to perfect. Striving for perfection is great, however, attaining greatness when starting out is highly unlikely.

For example, in the last paragraph I mention using a thumbnail design that incorporated a white background. After continued studying and testing, it became apparent that using a white background in a thumbnail design was not optimal on YouTube. After all, the YouTube website itself is white. Today, my primary "YouTube" thumbnails incorporate a red background, white lettering, and make use of shadows and strokes. The result is they really pop and they grab attention. I could have easily removed the wording around my "white background misstep." However, I wanted to leave it with the hopes that you can see that we all grow and nobody creates an amazing channel experience out of the gate.

Again, that is a great goal to strive for. However, YouTube is truly a journey and an art—one that takes time to improve upon.

Also, I often use images of my dogs and a mobile phone in certain thumbnails. Together, these elements create a style and as I made more videos focused on thumbnails, I increased my chances for showing up not once in search and Suggested Videos, but multiple times.

Plus, it's more fun, don't you think? The "SEO for YouTube" always incorporates red and black text, the background is pure white, and sometimes I add in my catchword, "MOAR." It's tongue-in-cheek and again creates a style and look. This style leverages two colors, and I sometimes outline myself in white, so it pops on YouTube.

Literally, as I was writing this section about creating a memorable channel and brand, this comment came in, another YouTuber who digs my silly, tongue-in-cheek sense of humor.

Thumbnails That Win the Click

- Less is Moar (a few words and a picture is great)

- Contrasting colors for the win
- Different is better than better
- Design for a tiny image
- Include your logo/profile picture
- Leverage the power of playlist congruency

Example of a Thumbnail That Works

My goal with each thumbnail is to identify **one or two central words** in the search term that I'm targeting and to draw attention to those words. In the above example, the video title is the same as the search term I'm targeting: *How to Get More Clicks on YouTube*.

The central word is "**Click**," so my thumbnail incorporates two very large words, one of them being "**Click**." Exactly what people are searching for. If I were to incorporate the entire search term, nothing would stand out. Furthermore, the video title is displayed in text right next to the thumbnail on YouTube. Here's what that thumbnail looks like in the search results. Talk about POP!

You can see that my thumbnail is fun and different. It's eye-catching and easy to read. My brand colors and logo are congruent. It's engaging (duh). It makes viewers want to "CLICK THIS"!

The following image shows the search results for "YouTube Keyword Tool."

My thumbnail contains three words, only one of which is contained in the target keyword phrase. However, that one word is highlighted in red and the other words are black. I think someone searching for "YouTube Keyword Tool" would get it. Once again, the thumbnail is different from the others listed and it pops. Of course, I may be biased.

SIDE NOTE: To fast track your results, focus on only two playlists until you've published videos that are driving views in each playlist. Videos driving views will push additional views to other videos in the playlist, which in time will result in more search results for more of your videos. This is much more powerful, and it creates momentum rather than publishing various videos on many different topics.

Let's review what you've learned so far. The way to get noticed on YouTube is to create not only great looking thumbnails and graphics, but to leverage the power of congruency, playlists, and to go deep on various topics.

If you've got a vlog-style channel, you can do this by theming your video content into playlists. What we've covered here is not terribly hard. You simply need to take the time to plan it out, something that most struggling YouTubers don't do. t

Free YouTube Starter Kit

Drive More Views with my
12-Step Upload Checklist
(Can Be Integrated into Tubebuddy)

Convert More Views with My

End Screen Templates
Access: BrianGJohnson.TV/Free

CHAPTER FIVE

Answer the Why

Make It Easy for People to Understand *Why*

Imagine that each new viewer who accesses your channel has one *burning question* that you must address. That question is, "What do I get in exchange for my time watching your videos by subscribing?"

Imagine that these viewers are not overly interested, impressed, or even attentive. You've literally got a second or two to address their question and make a favorable impression. Do that, and you'll be rewarded with another subscriber. This is why creating a visually striking brand and channel is powerful. It makes an impression in milliseconds and results in people wanting to further explore your channel.

Information Wars

Whether a viewer is watching a video they just clicked on or checking out your channel page, more often than not they make like Nicolas Cage and are gone in sixty seconds. Truth be told, it's probably more accurate to say they're gone in three seconds, but then I wouldn't have gotten to use the Nick Cage reference. But I digress . . .

Viewers may leave quickly unless you make a strong case for why they should stick around and check out what you have to offer. This is why you must *make it easy* for viewers to identify that your channel and/or video offers something they're not going to want to miss.

What are they getting in exchange for their time? Hopefully, engaging content and a reason to return. In the previous chapter, we already began to take steps to make sure that happens. Ask yourself these questions:

- What makes your channel cool?
- What makes your channel unique and different?
- What will your channel offer that can't be found elsewhere?
- Why should people care and subscribe?

Think about that last one: Why should people care about your channel? After all, there are more than a bazillion channels available to viewers on YouTube. What makes yours special? These are not easy questions to answer; however, by asking yourself now, what makes my channel unique, different, and worthy of subscribing, you're ultimately tasking your brain to come up with answers to the age-old question: *why*?

Why Should They Subscribe?

Ask yourself the following questions right now and out loud:

- What makes my channel different?
- What makes my channel unique?
- Why should people subscribe?

The goal is not to simply answer these questions, but to **articulate the why in less time, with fewer words**. Because when you do that, you make it easy for the viewer to understand why.

We've become a society of ADHD and OCD and otherwise distracted humans who are constantly scrolling, clicking, and wondering about this, that, and the other. We live in a world of too much information! Most of us suffer from information overload, and as a result, we never find the information we truly want or need.

What was once valuable, that is, access to information, has now become a curse. People used to buy encyclopedias to gain information, today we have the Internet. Google, Facebook, YouTube, and a million other sites are all filled with tremendous information that most of us will never see.

The problem is that most of the information available to us is crap (a technical term). People must sift, sort, and wade through mountains of videos, status updates, emails, white papers, blog posts, and more!

You have a better chance of rising above the noise if you understand that the most precious thing someone can give you is their time.

So, it's imperative that you take the time to *make it easy for viewers* to understand *why* they should give some of their precious time to you. The sooner they get it, the better. Remember: brevity, repetition, and striking visuals for the win.

Building a Better Mousetrap

The first few chapters of this book discussed how to create a memorable channel that stands out, makes a statement, and drives more views.

This chapter will guide you through the process of **converting more viewers into subscribers**. It's about taking the time to strategize how to build a better mousetrap before the construction begins, i.e., before viewers land on your channel page.

It's important to understand how the conversion process works (or doesn't). How do YouTube viewers become your YouTube subscribers? Often, that process begins with what's called "The Video Watch Page."

Video Watch Page

Look at the image below. The red arrow points to a red and white "subscribe" button that viewers can click to subscribe. The black arrow points to the link that takes viewers to that YouTuber's channel page. Viewers tend to check out a channel by clicking the channel link before deciding whether to subscribe.

Now let's look at my channel analytics for a moment. The following image details subscribers gained over the last twenty-eight days.

Notice "channel" gained 859 subscribers, while "video" gained a total of 309 subscribers. This is of critical importance, and here's why: As a viewer watches one of your videos, they may ask themselves if they should subscribe. Rather than deciding while watching your video, most viewers will click your channel link to help them make this important decision.

Let's dig into this. If they clicked to your channel page, chances are that your video offered value in some way and they liked it! KABOOM! Nice work! You have them on the hook. Now it's time to seal the deal by converting the viewer into a subscriber. Many YouTubers totally drop the ball and never take the time to create that *first awesome impression*, thus the percentage of viewers who visit their channel page and become subscribers is very low. This one step greatly impacts how fast your channel will grow. As mentioned earlier, those in my niche vary greatly when it comes to converting viewers into subscribers. The difference is as much as four times! Meaning, for every 1,000 viewers, one channel converts four times as many viewers into subscribers.

Know this: Viewers to your channel page will expend little effort in assessing the value your channel offers. If you're so lucky to have inspired someone to click and visit your channel, close the deal and inspire them to become a subscriber by creating a visually striking channel page that:

- Is easily understood
- Inspires further action

If your channel looks great, they'll either hit the subscribe button or they'll watch another video. If, however, your channel fails to impress them, chances are good that your viewer-to-subscriber ratio will be greatly reduced. This is why you see, hear, and experience a company's brand (as well as their value proposition) again and again and again.

- Think different!
- Melts in your mouth, not in your hand!
- Just do it!
- It's finger lickin' good!

Of course, what we're talking about is great branding. Not just branding, mind you, but *great* branding. The easier you make it for people to remember and talk about you, the more they'll talk.

Finger lickin' good, melts in your mouth, just do it. Your mind is branded by their repetitive messaging. You see, hear and experience the same icons, slogans, value proportions, visuals, colors, and audio cues again and again. As we encounter something repeatedly, the more likely we are to remember it.

You also want your brand (and YouTube channel) to be unique and different so that it stands out from the crowd. For example, just between you and me, if I asked someone in the entrepreneurial space what they did, and they replied, "I'm an author, speaker, and online entrepreneur," I would yawn, seriously. That's not memorable because so many people use the same exact words on their website, social media graphics, and more. Ask me what I do, and I'll tell you:

> ***"I help people amplify their message."***

That sums up what I do. It's unique, it's short, and it's to the point. If you ask those who watch my videos about me, they might mention my dogs, how fun I am, expressive and goofy. They might mention that I say "pixie dust" in my videos or that I'm the world's first poodle wrangler. These items are fun, different, and unique to my brand, and they make *it easy for* people to remember me. Of course, I bring to the table the very results that people are after, which helps cement my value proposition to them.

This book is a great example of that. It's based on how I jump-started my YouTube channel, increased my views by 439 percent, and grew a large subscriber base quickly. That's what they get in exchange for their time.

Spark Interest & Make a Statement Visually

The point is this: The quickest way to make a statement and peak the viewer's interest is to leverage the power of great YouTube channel art, thumbnails, and design.

We've already established that you don't need to spend a fortune or be a graphic designer to create a brand that draws viewers in.

Popular YouTuber JackSepticEye comes to mind (see image next page). Jack came up with a clever and different channel name and has unique channel art that well represents his brand. It's simple branding that's also incredibly memorable and effective. This is a great example of the power of simplicity.

Jack's brand colors are shades of green. His hair is green, his channel art is green, and his profile picture is green. Notice that Jack uses a logo for his YouTube profile picture that could be easily be integrated into his thumbnails for congruency.

However, at 12.4 million subscribers, Jack does not need any tips or advice from me. Jack, like all highly successful YouTubers, creates highly engaging videos that are fun and different and get lots of watch time. Do that incredibly well, and the rest does not matter.

Channel Art

Notice that Jack's channel art contains no words other than his name and the "eye logo." Less is so much more.

If your channel art is cluttered with words, arrows pointing to the subscribe button, social media graphics, the days which you publish and more, it may confuse viewers, or at least make it harder for them to understand what your channel is about.

Remember, new viewers to your channel are going to spend just a few seconds looking things over. Make it easy for them to understand what they get in exchange for their time, and you'll win the click!

Making It Easy-Tube Ritual Customization

So, the lesson is to make it easy for viewers to understand what you offer. Creating simple, congruent channel art, and thumbnails is a great way to do just that. However, there are a few other things you can do to ensure that you make it dead simple for viewers to understand the value you bring to the table.

One of the best ways to do that is to customize your channel. This is how you control exactly what visitors to your channel page see. If you don't customize your channel, visitors may see a feed of your most recent viewing activities rather than your actual videos. That means that someone else's video will show up on your feed as a clickable link to their channel. You're inviting potential subscribers to leave your page! That's committing YouTube suicide!

That's right, if you don't customize your channel page, your YouTube activity will result in links to other videos and channels posted on your page. To make sure that doesn't happen, you must customize your channel page so that it converts more viewers into your subscribers, not someone else's.

Channel Customization (Browse Mode)

To customize your channel, log in to your YouTube account and click *My Channel* in the left menu (this is the page visitors and subscribers see). On the right side of the page, near the subscribe button, click the gear icon to access channel customization options.

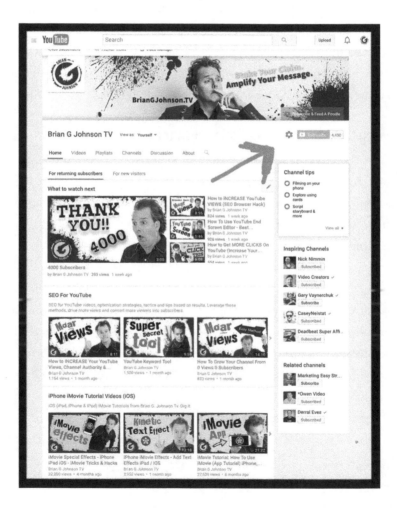

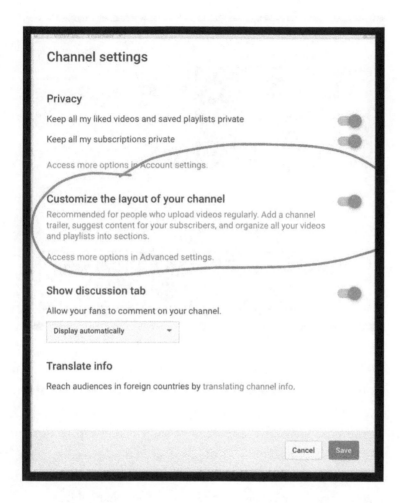

Clicking the gear icon opens the channel settings page shown below.

Enable channel customization by clicking the slider to the on position. Also note on this page you can keep your YouTube activity private if you like.

After you've enabled channel customization, the top section of your channel will be replaced with a section that's designed

for both returning subscribers and new visitors to your channel. In the image below, notice the page is set to "returning visitors" and features the four most recent videos uploaded to the channel.

In the next image, we're looking at the channel top section once again. However, instead of "returning subscribers" the section is set for "new visitors." In other words, viewers who have not subscribed to your channel will see this view once they land on your channel page.

Even better, you can configure both the "returning subscribers" and "new visitor" sections as you see fit. Notice, I have a channel trailer video active in the new visitor section.

To configure the video content that you want to be displayed in either of these sections, simply click on the "pen" (edit) icon to the right of these sections as displayed in the image below.

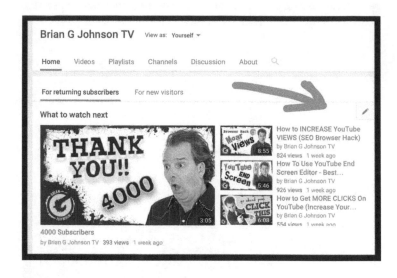

Configuring the Top Channel Panel

Here are my thoughts on how you may want to configure these two sections for best results.

Returning Subscribers

The default setting for returning subscribers is to show your most recent video in the large video display section (as pictured in the image on the previous page). I think this makes the most sense because you want returning visitors to see your latest videos. Chances are they will find something in this top section that they have not seen. So, I leave this as it is. However, you can select one video that you always want to be featured for this section.

New Visitors & Channel Trailers

This top panel allows YouTube channel creators the chance to make a specific video that welcomes new visitors to their channel. Before I continue, let me share what I feel is an important distinction about how you create and publish content to YouTube, online, and in general.

The Bad Boy Ritual-Breaking the Rules

In the coming pages, I'm going to share what I learned about channel trailers, best practices, and optimization. You know, all the *rules* we should follow to "optimize" our channels.

However, creating content online is a creative process. If you create and publish content, that's creative. Just how creative you take it is up to you. How you update your Facebook status, creative videos, or optimize your YouTube channel is an opportunity for you to do it in a *fun, creative, and different* manner.

Those last few words, mind you, are what separates highly successful channels from those that generate average results. This is where things become a bit blurred.

Very often ***fun, creative, and different*** do not fit into a well-optimized machine like YouTube, which for many is the very thing they are looking for.

I can't tell you how many times I've been asked:

- What's the best way to make money online?
- What's the best way to publish an ebook?
- What's the best way to optimize a YouTube channel?

Of course, the answer is different for everyone based on their skills, abilities, talents, how often they've practiced their craft, and more. Furthermore, it's incredibly important to examine what success means to you. For me, right now, I want to grow my channel exponentially, as well as my email subscriber base. However, I also find it to be just as important to do it in a fun and creative way.

To do it my way.

Today, at fifty years of age, I like to learn the rules of the game and then move forward and do it my way.

The decisions I make, i.e., how willing I am to break "best practices" in all areas of my creative expression, are based on being creative *and* achieving success. Both are critically important to me at this stage of the game.

For example, my brain tells me that the first few seconds of my current channel trailer are not in line with my own best practices. The first few seconds do not show my face, are a bit slow, and may be costing me a few subscribers. However, my channel trailer is very creative, very different, and I like it.

The first few seconds feature a fun and quirky song. Heck the name of the song is something like "happy and quirky."

The video is edited to the beat of the song, with my logo popping in. Fun, fun, fun! From that point, the video is in alignment with best practices.

I welcome new viewers to my channel and share a bit about what my channel offers and what a subscriber can count on. The video is unique and different. That makes it memorable. That's why it's called "Subscribe and Feed a Poodle."

I think it's a solid trailer for sure, but not perfectly optimized, and I'm okay with that. To fully optimize the video per my own best practices, I might lose some of the quirky, creative spark that makes what I do creative and fun, or in other words, what makes me me!

If you focus on what YouTube considers to be the most important measure of success, i.e., creating engaging videos that keep viewers watching and coming back for more, you'll win, even if you break a few rules along the way.

After all, that's why YouTube viewers return to the platform—to be engaged, entertained, and sometimes to even learn a thing or two.

The moral of the story is to not go overboard with optimization at the expense of losing all creativity. Find a happy medium and understand that not everybody is going to dig what you do. That's okay, especially if you create to please yourself, first and foremost.

Here's what I've discovered about channel trailers.

The First Ten Seconds Is Key

In the first ten seconds of your channel trailer, you'll want to be in the frame and welcoming visitors to your channel. I start with, "Hey! It's me! Brian G, welcome to Brian G TV."

- Welcome viewers
- Introduce yourself

Next, let *potential* subscribers know what they can expect and address the "what's in it for me?" question. The easier you make it for people to understand the value your channel offers, the better. Simple words and short sentences make it easier for viewers to understand why they should subscribe. Don't let your ego get in the way. Don't talk over the head of viewers just to make yourself sound more important. Again, less is more.

Keep in mind that viewers who don't already know, like, and trust you have the attention span of a gnat. Brevity for the win!

My channel trailer mentions within the first forty-five seconds that Brian G Johnson TV (channel name) is all about, "*inspiring action in other people and that anything worthwhile begins when others act on the content you publish. Whether that's a video you publish to YouTube, a book you publish, or maybe you want to build a list or sell a product. Anything worthwhile begins when you inspire action.*"

The core of my value proposition is to "Amplify & Inspire Action!" Those words are featured in my channel art, and I mention them in most of my videos. It's the phrase I repeat to make it easy for people to remember me. Furthermore, it's also the thing that many people want to learn how to do for their own YouTube channel.

They want to:

- Inspire viewers to subscribe.
- Inspire people to opt into a list.
- Inspire people to share their content.
- Inspire people to buy a product or service.

Next, I talk about how I *inspire people*, not just by sharing my message, but by *amplifying it*. It's what I teach on my channel: *amplified messages inspire action*. This is the "what's in it for me?" part of the trailer.

What do you get in exchange for your time? *You'll discover how to not just share your message online, but how to amplify it in order to inspire people to act.*

This is me, pitching my channel, addressing the "what's in it for me?" and "why should I subscribe?" questions right off the bat.

Side Note: The more clearly you can articulate why someone should subscribe, and do so in the shortest amount of time, the better your results will be. You get bonus points for making your channel trailer different, unique, and memorable.

How Often Do I Publish New Videos?

Next, you want to let potential subscribers know how often you publish. Many experts recommend creating a publishing schedule and sticking to it come hell or high water. I don't adhere to a schedule, so I just say, "I publish new videos often, and you should subscribe so you never miss one." Over the last six months or so, I've published, on average, several times a week to as much as seven times a week.

I like the idea of a regular schedule. It's powerful and helps keep everyone on track, especially the video creator. However, what's more powerful than a regular schedule that results in say eight videos in a month? A mindset and goal that results in ten, twelve, or even as many as twenty videos in a month. This is exactly why I abandoned a schedule after a few months. My volume increased because I ended up doing more videos than I would have if I'd committed to a set schedule.

I wanted to make it simple for me to publish more often. I felt that publishing more videos over time would outweigh having a set schedule.

Seven months into my case study, and with 121 video uploads behind me, my intuition tells me I made a good choice. We'll cover more on publishing frequency in the coming pages.

Less Than Ninety Seconds in Total

As with most things, when it comes to a channel trailer, less is more. The more clearly you can articulate why someone should subscribe, and in the shortest amount of time, the better your results will be. I know, I've said that before, but it bears repeating.

Channel Trailer Recommended, But Not Required

Just because YouTube crafted the channel layout to allow video creators to publish a channel trailer does not mean you should have or need one. This is especially true if you're just getting started, or if you're trying to jump-start your channel and have yet to publish a channel trailer.

Instead, you may wish to include one of your better performing videos (when it comes to converting viewers into subscribers) in the channel trailer position. Doing this allows you to focus on creating videos that will serve your audience over the long term, while also targeting a specific search term.

Last, understand that including a regular video in the channel trailer position, that is the video that you select for new visitors, is a great way to **drive more views to that video**, which can help it accumulate more watch time and drive better search results.

CHAPTER SIX

Convert Viewers into Subscribers

So far, we've focused most of our energy on crafting a channel that will convert more YouTube viewers into YouTube subscribers. Now it's time to focus our attention on individual videos, ensuring that each video we publish drives more views and does a good job at converting viewers into subscribers.

What's exciting about what I'm going to share is that small changes that don't take a lot of additional effort can have a huge impact on your ability to convert. It's all about creating not just a call to action, but a fun and engaging call to action, and that's what we'll focus on in this chapter.

The Most Important Thing

As I began to outline this section, I thought about just how important it is to point out the elephant in the room. It is the number one factor that separates YouTube winners from YouTube losers.

It's the thing that, when you get it right, success happens no matter what. That is, even if you pay no attention to keywords, titles, thumbnails, and all the other important elements, you'd still crush it. On the other side of the coin, if you fail in this area, you will struggle.

Unlearn Boring

The most powerful YouTube software is the thing between your ears. How you think and view the world is different from how other people do because we all have experienced life on our terms, only as we could have experienced it.

When you begin to ask yourself, what makes my channel different, or why should people subscribe, you begin to exercise creative thinking.

The cool thing about creativity is that you never lose your ability to be creative. However, sometimes you may feel that you're being judged by others (or you fear being judged) and you begin to play it safe. Creativity suffers because you're sensitive to the judgment of others.

I've always been a little quirky. I've always been a little different. While I never tried to hide that, I never used my quirks to my advantage. Somewhere around 2013, I began to realize that the things that make me seem weird in some people's eyes also make me powerful in the eyes of others. I stopped worrying (actually, to say that I worried less is more accurate) about what others might think of me and started being me, in all my flawed and quirky glory. It's become part of my brand and one of the things that makes my videos memorable.

This doesn't mean you need to act a fool or go overboard in your videos. It does mean that sometimes taking a risk and doing something unexpected can generate great rewards.

I first heard the phrase "**unlearn boring**" from author Sally Hogshead. It spoke to me because somewhere along the way, so many of us learned that it's better to play it safe. Today, as I type this, the idea of playing it safe scares the heck out of me, because I don't want to play it safe with the content I create. For me, the idea of truly blending education and entertainment gets me excited. Sure, it takes courage and effort, but it sure is worth it!

Many successful YouTubers found success by playing by their own rules, with the goal of creating something that was unique and different. Being different often plays a big role when it comes to creating engaging content. Being different, or creating content that is different, makes you unique and helps you rise above the noise. It is a pathway that has led to so much success in numerous fields, not just YouTube. So, fly that freak flag and share what's on the inside. You dig?

Optimized for YouTube-Ritual Video Structure

Look at the most successful YouTube creators and you'll see that there's a structure that's followed in nearly every video they do. That structure is rather simple: *Beginning – Middle – End.*

Make sure your videos stick to this proven formula:

- Create an introduction that hooks viewers in at the beginning of your video.
- Deliver the value that you promised with your YouTube thumbnail and video title in the middle of your video.

- After you delivered the value you promised, create a call to action that will result in more subscribers or more people viewing more of your videos.

Ultimately, how effective you are in each of these three sections will determine the success of your YouTube channel.

Intro: Video Title + Thumbnail + 15-Second Hook

The first minute of a YouTube video is extremely important. Strike that; it's ***mission critical***. If you haven't studied YouTube video analytics, then you may not be aware that a huge percentage of viewers will stop watching a video within the first minute. Abandonment rates that run as high as 50 to 70 percent in the first minute are not uncommon.

However, there are many things that you can do to greatly improve the audience retention rate of your videos, which as you know by now, is the very thing that YouTube rewards; that is, videos that keep people watching longer.

In the first fifteen seconds of my video, my goal is to draw attention to the focus keyword(s). Earlier, I talked about not just identifying a keyword phrase to target, but rather the words within the keyword phrase that separate it from other similar keyword phrases.

- **Example:** YouTube Keyword *Tool*
- **Example:** YouTube Keyword *Research*

Both keyword phrases are very similar. Yet, for someone who's extremely interested in keywords, they're also very different. One phrase deals with identifying a *tool* that can be used to help someone gain results, while the other search phrase is based on learning how to move forward and conduct *research*. They are similar keyword phrases that have a different connotation for those interested in the topics. This is where things get exciting, so stick with me.

In the above example, I created two videos that each targeted both keyword phrases. Let's look at how I crafted my video title, thumbnail, and the intro of the "tool" video. The title to the video was *YouTube Keyword Tool.*

Author's Note: Above is one of my older white background thumbnails. It looks great in a book, it would look great against a dark background, but on YouTube it does not draw the eye like my revamped "red" thumbnails. On the next page, I have included my revised thumbnail.

The Video Hook Ritual

The following four steps allow me to craft engaging videos time and again. Ideally, I run through these four steps prior to stepping in front of a camera so I know exactly what my focus is for the video and specifically mention it at the introduction of the video.

Step 1: Identify Video Topic

I think this speaks for itself. Before you begin, figure out what topic you'll be covering in the video (duh).

Step 2: Identify Target Keyword Phrase

In this step, I identify the *exact keyword phrase* I'm going to target for this video. This is extremely helpful because once I know the exact keywords I'm targeting, I can mention those words in the video itself, which helps keep more people watching, which brings us to Step 3.

Step 3: Identify Focus Keyword(s)

Next, I select one or two *focus keywords* from the main keyword phrase itself. In our example, the keyword phrase I'm targeting is: YouTube Keyword *Tool.*

In this example, the focus keyword is clearly *tool*. It's the one word that separates this phrase from other similar keyword phrases people are searching for on YouTube.

Step 4: Spotlight Thumbnail

In the previous steps, we identified our target keyword phrase and took it a step further by identifying the focus keyword. With this information in mind, we can now focus our efforts on drawing attention to the "most important" keyword(s). Step 4 is to craft a video thumbnail that draws the eye to our focus word. In this case, the word is *tool*.

In the thumbnail image above, I've put a spotlight on the world *tool* by using yellow for that word. Note, yellow is one of my brand colors and thus ties nicely in with my logo. Also, the whole keyword phrase I'm targeting is "YouTube Keyword Tool," and this will be the exact title of my video.

So, right next to my thumbnail viewers will see the exact keyword phrase (title) that they were searching for. Combine that with an awesome thumbnail designed to catch their eye, and you win the click. Notice that I didn't incorporate the entire keyword phrase into my thumbnail. I like to craft thumbnails that entice a click. My thumbnail alludes to the fact that I'm going to share a "*super-secret tool.*"

That's far more intriguing than simply featuring the keywords I'm targeting on the thumbnail. This also allows me to further develop my brand, style, and messaging.

Step 5: Verbally Mention Focus Keyword(s) in the First Fifteen Seconds

So far, we've made it easy for a potential viewer to want to click on our Thumbnail when searching for anything related to the search phrase *YouTube Keyword Tool.*

We've included the search term in our video title and crafted a thumbnail that is eye-catching and easy to understand. Now it's time to seal the deal by hooking the viewer because if you do these things correctly, you'll get clicks.

At a minimum, mention the focus keyword(s) within the first fifteen seconds of your video. You get bonus points if you're able to incorporate the entire keyword phrase that you're targeting in those first fifteen seconds.

To review, here are the five steps of my creation ritual:

- **Step 1**: Identify the video topic.
- **Step 2**: Identify the target keyword phrase.
- **Step 3**: Select one or two *focus* words from the keyword phrase.
- **Step 4**: Create an awesome thumbnail using the focus keyword.
- **Step 5**: Verbally mention focus words with the first fifteen seconds of the video.

Here's how I started out the first fifteen seconds of this video:

- "Imagine, a keyword tool that told you what you should rank for!"

I mentioned the phrase "keyword tool" within the first five seconds. Hook! I then cut to a screen capture with me sharing the very result someone who is interested in learning about "keyword tools" would be interested in—that is, a top-ten YouTube search ranking.

This is extremely powerful, and I'll tell you why. What I'm addressing right off the bat are the results that a YouTube searcher is most likely going after beyond their immediate search term.

The search term is based on a *tool* that will help with keyword research. However, is that what they really want? I think it's safe to say that the real desire is to rank highly in YouTube search and to drive views.

I also mentioned the word *imagine*, which puts the searcher in a place of them thinking about the kind of results I'm generating and how they can too.

- "Imagine, a keyword tool that told you what you should rank for!"

Just try this tactic yourself, and if you do, let me know how it worked out for you! Feel free to tag me on Facebook! This is super-powerful because you're identifying (on a deeper level) the needs and wants of people who are searching for and finding your content.

Make It Fun & Engaging

Incorporating music, fun editing, cool effects, cracking a joke, a slight raise of your eyebrow, or adding something that's not expected is a great way to add an element of engagement to your video. I'll also mention timing. They say one of the elements of a great comedian is their timing. The same is true on YouTube. Knowing when to pause, when to speed up your cadence, and when to insert a sound effect will come with practice. Even if you're teaching, focus on delivering your message in an engaging and entertaining manner, and it will pay off big.

Having a nice video background that gives viewers something to look at can add a bit more engagement to your video but can also be distracting. There are so many ways to create engagement, and it's something you can easily do.

You might be thinking, hey, Brian G, that's great for you, but I'm just not that funny. Humor is just one way to create engagement. You can create engagement in many ways (educate, entertain, teach, etc.).

Typically, those YouTubers who have the greatest success keep viewers engaged by entertaining them in some shape, form, or fashion. You can even use visual tricks and clever editing to hold engagement. At the twenty-two-second point of the *tool* video, I cut to a new angle, flash to black and white, and I tweaked the audio in Final Cut Pro to sound slightly different.

I do this to make it easy for the viewers to know that something has changed. In this shot, I assume the role of a character I often use in my video called "The Cowhand" and I ask, "Hey, boss, what about a tablet, like an iPad?"

The video then cuts back to the previous angle, full color, and audio quality, where I answer by saying, "You bet you can access this tool on an iPad!" That's me, creating something fun and different that fits with my brand. Hopefully, viewers find it engaging. My statistics show that they do. Access and watch the video so you can see how this works.

☐ BrianGJohnson.tv/trv1/tool

Over the first minute of the video, I include two calls to action (one to like the video and another reminding the viewer to subscribe). I roll my brand intro and include my value proposition to ensure the viewer will gain some value by not only watching this video but by subscribing and watching some of my other videos as well. I focus 60 percent of my energy on creating a solid first minute. The result has been excellent because after you've hooked a viewer in the first minute, you don't have to work as hard to keep them watching. You simply deliver the value you promised to win the click.

Video Play by Play

1. First 10 Seconds—"Keyword Tool" Focus Keyword
2. 10 to 16 Seconds—Proof/What They Want
3. 18 Seconds—CTA (Smash the Like Button)
4. 16 to 22 Seconds—Imagine Statement #2
5. 22 to 26 Seconds—Cowhand—Fun, Engaging, Different
6. 27 Seconds—Answers to Cowhand—More Details on Secret Tool
7. 30 to 35 Seconds—Imagine Statement #3 (Free)
8. 37 Seconds—Super Secret Statement (Thumbnail Correlation)
9. 43 Seconds—End Intro/Dig It (Engaging)
10. 44 Seconds—Call to Action—Fun & Different Subscribe
11. 45 Seconds—Brand Intro
12. 52 Seconds—Value Proposition—How to Inspire Action
13. 1:03—Value Proposition—Inspire Action = More Subs

Before we move on to the middle section of the video, I want to emphasize a few points.

1: Top Priority Is to Keep the Viewer Watching

The priority is to focus on the needs and wants of the viewer first, because if you take care of their needs, they'll be more likely to keep watching. This can improve watch time and retention, which can lead to better rankings and garner YouTube's help in promoting the video in search and Suggested Videos.

I don't recommend starting your video off immediately with a snazzy intro (if you use one). The viewer doesn't care about your intro.

Viewers want the value that your video thumbnail and title promised, and they want it NOW.

They don't want to see your name streak across the screen in a ball of fire. Later, after hooking the viewer, then focus on the calls to action, mention subscribing, and take care of your needs. Mix this up, and you'll hurt your overall results.

2: Engagement-Different Is Better Than Better

It's so incredibly satisfying to unexpectedly discover something new and fresh, something different. Perhaps it's a great movie or TV show. I can remember watching a special on MTV about the first *Matrix* movie. In its day, the movie was unique and different, and I remember calling my girlfriend at the time (who's now my wife) and telling her that we needed to go see this movie right away. The story was so unique and different. It pulled me in and I kept watching. I wanted to see what would happen next. I wanted to learn more about this strange and different universe and the characters who lived in it. It was, in a word, engaging.

That's the power of "different," and with video, you can easily create your own style, brand, look, and feel that are different from what's already on YouTube. Doing so will give you an edge. What's awesome is that you don't have to have everything figured out before getting started.

I think lots of video creators "plan out" their channel to death and never end up uploading video. Some planning makes sense; however, know that most great YouTubers became great YouTubers by creating different, unique, engaging videos recorded in their unique voice and style, then honing things along the way. The sooner you get started, the sooner you can begin to polish and hone your skills. Just remember: Different is better than same old.

3: Style & Substance

Your videos must have substance (something of value to give the viewer in exchange for their time). If you're a gamer or vlogger, you still must offer value in your videos or viewers will not stick around. You need to be able to tell a story and to entertain. Nearly anything can be made into a story, a daily vlog, a training tutorial, a gaming segment, or perhaps even a twenty-second clip of you just stuck in traffic.

Engaging stories offer substance, just like a great tutorial, one that doesn't tell the viewer what to do but shows them how to do it. Combine engagement and substance, and you'll win.

Hooking the viewer early is the first step, one that many YouTubers never figure out how to do. Next, the goal becomes adding value by delivering substance. Let's dive into how to add value in a unique way.

Add Substance & Deliver Promised Value

How exactly can you add value, style, and substance? The following describes how I do it.

1: Show Them

I've had numerous people tell me they loved my videos because:

- "You didn't tell me what to do, you showed me. Even better, you showed me step by step, and it was backed up by results!"

This is an easy way to add substance and value to your video. Show, don't tell.

2: Clarity for the Win

If you are teaching viewers how to do something that you have done with amazing results (like ranking videos high on YouTube), and you fail to clearly communicate how you achieved those results, your watch time (and perhaps your credibility) will suffer. Anytime I release training videos, I take the time to clearly communicate how the results were achieved. Sometimes people mention that my training is a bit slow or that there's too much of it. However, more often than not, people appreciate the fact that I took the time to make something easy to understand.

As I'm writing this, a great example just popped into my mind. Years ago, when I began teaching SEO, I tried to share and teach every little detail that I spent many years learning. I shared the big picture, as well as the small nuances of search engine optimization.

This information was complete and in-depth, but much of it was over the heads of those just getting started with SEO, who had a hard time grasping the concepts I was teaching. As I began to create my third product in 2009, I began to appreciate and understand the value of a checklist, a formula, a blueprint, and the words "step by step." As a result, I became a much better teacher.

Taking a complex subject like SEO and breaking it down into a formula or a series of steps makes it easier for people to believe that they can learn to do what you're teaching. That's powerful stuff to know if your videos are meant to teach and educate the viewer.

Perhaps in your life you've struggled with some subject matter until you found the right teacher, and then everything clicked. When that happens, you remember and appreciate the person who made it possible for you to move forward with the task at hand. Clarity for the win.

Take the time to simplify what you're sharing. You can do this by creating formulas, creating videos based on listed items, or creating a step-by-step system. This very book takes a multiple-step ritual and breaks it down into smaller steps that are easy to understand. I've done this time and again because it works.

3: Brevity Saves the Day

If you can say and communicate the same things in a four-minute video rather than a six-minute video, then the perfect video length (for that particular video) is four minutes. Being repetitive will hurt your retention and, to a degree, your ability to rank videos on YouTube.

As you begin to grow a subscriber base, those people will listen to you for longer periods of time and will give you leeway when it comes to brevity.

Why? Because you've established a relationship with your subscriber base. Subscribers watch longer because they know, like, and trust you. That's why channels with large subscriber bases are so powerful. It's the reason why subscribers watch an average of 25 percent longer than nonsubscribers.

Structure your videos based on what I'm outlining here, and you'll be more likely to hook nonsubscribers into watching your videos. Bottom line, your videos should only be as long as they need to be. Brevity for the win.

4: Your Unique & Different Viewpoint

People value unique points of view that are brought to their attention in a unique and entertaining way. For example, I've been a gamer for most of my life. As I've been writing this book, a new game is being released based on World War I.

Interestingly, some of the most successful YouTubers who have released videos based on this game have created different and unique videos that were tied to this game, but ultimately shared their unique viewpoints of what we may see in the game. In other words, they created videos based on their perspective and what they thought of the game.

For example, one YouTuber created a video covering what types of unusual weapons might be featured in the game. Another YouTuber shared how the usage of army rations was something that happened around World War I. He went on to create his own hypothetical meal rations that were based on what soldiers were eating around World War I.

This is something that becomes even more powerful as you gain subscribers, because those subscribers become very interested in how *you* think, and they help spread your ideas by sharing your videos. Videos that are different from the status quo have higher engagement levels. Videos that share a unique and different perspective provide the answer to the question I asked earlier, *What's in it for me?* You get a unique point of view on a topic that interests you. That's a win.

Don't be afraid to share your point of view in your unique style because that's one of the things that makes you you. Especially when you're just starting out, after all, you have very little to lose and everything to gain.

5: A Deeper Sense of Value

If a YouTube viewer is searching for something such as "YouTube keyword tool," then this topic, and your ability to deliver value regarding a *YouTube keyword tool,* is the priority.

However, there are many things that all human beings want, beyond their immediate needs. If you're able to satisfy the viewer's needs and wants when it comes to the priority, then you also can offer even more value.

Example, as you're sharing information about a YouTube tool, making someone smile or laugh is a bonus. It's extra stuff that the viewers get on top of what they came for. Free laughs all around, Cowhand!

Making someone laugh or smile is good stuff, for sure. Providing hope for someone struggling is value without question. Editing videos in a unique and different style may be the very thing that separates your videos from similar channels.

When I began Brian G Johnson TV, I knew I wanted my quirkiness and onscreen antics to be part of my brand. I also knew I wanted to dive in deep and not just tell viewers things, but show them how to do things to get proven results. I'll mention that it took a bunch of videos to figure out how to blend that quirky Brian G style with delivering "how-to" information. I knew where I was headed, and I kept trying. As I created the first few dozen videos, I tried different things to see what worked and what didn't. I was not afraid to experiment with any aspect of the process. Somewhere around the fiftieth video or so, everything just clicked. I found my voice and style, and it has paid off for me ever since.

Thus, as you move forward, understand that often you can't simply plan a lot of these things out. Rather they come with practice, they come with experimentation, and by having the courage to try different things. People don't fail. They simply give up before the magic happens.

The End: Call to Action

Now we've reached the end of the video, and it's our turn to make a pitch (call to action). We've delivered the goods to the viewer. Now it's their turn to show us a little love.

The pitch could include any of the following:

- Subscribe
- Like and/or share the video
- Comment on the video
- Visit the associated website
- Email opt-in (giveaway/access/download)
- Watch another video
- Follow me on (social site)

Once again, less is more, lots more.

A common mistake that many YouTubers make is to mention multiple calls to action at the end of their video. If you're pitching too many balls at a batter, chances are they may not hit a single one. Confuse or inundate the viewer, and the result may be that they take no action at all.

Have you ever found yourself standing in the ice cream aisle for several minutes, wondering which flavor or treat to select? In that moment, you may suffer from information overload as you try to process the hundreds of options. I think I've lost about four months of my life, standing and staring in the ice cream aisle.

However, give people a few choices and the decision process becomes much easier, which, if you remember, was one of the goals when creating our channel. Make it easy for the visitor to identify what makes your channel different, valuable, and worth subscribing to. Once again, the easier you make it for viewers, the better your results will be.

As you near the end of your video, you can greatly increase the percentage of viewers who take action based on your pitch. The more value you provide in your video content, the more likely viewers will subscribe, opt-in, or visit your website.

A few of the topics we covered earlier, clarity and brevity, will also help you increase your results no matter what you pitch at the end of your video.

Value Proposition

You should come up with a brief value proposition that clearly communicates what your channel offers the viewer in exchange for their time.

My value proposition is clear, concise, and to the point. I teach you how to: *Stake your claim, amplify your message, and inspire action—the very things that are needed for success.*

Ritual Tools: End Screen & Cards

YouTube offers several tools that you can use to make it easier for viewers to become subscribers, view more videos, or visit your website.

These tools include the following:

- YouTube cards
- YouTube end screen

Both YouTube cards and the YouTube end screen allows YouTube creators to add interactive clickable buttons into their videos that make it easy for viewers to subscribe, watch another video or playlist, visit an associated website, and poll viewers.

These tools are mobile friendly, which is awesome since many people watch on their smartphones or mobile devices.

YouTube Cards

As mentioned, YouTube cards make it possible to add clickable links to an associated website, video, playlist, and channel, and you can even poll subscribers.

A card can be added to a video at any point within the video. However, you can only add a total of three cards per video. In the previous image, I'm pointing to a YouTube card. In this video, I'm mentioning a previous video and saying that viewers may want to check it out. Using a YouTube card makes it super-easy to link between videos, channels, and playlists, which makes it easier for viewers to watch and take action.

You can also create a card that links to an associated website. Going in-depth about the associated website is beyond the scope of this guide. However, essentially an associated website is one that you link to in your YouTube account inside of Creator Studio. You verify the website and once that's done, you can then link to the associated website with both cards and end screens.

You can mention a free download, article, or product review that's available on your site, then add a card creating a clickable link within the video to that site. Super-powerful for list building! In the coming days, I'm going to add a card to each one of my videos that will offer a free ebook to viewers. Cards make adding that functionality simple and straightforward.

To Create a YouTube Card

To create a YouTube card, simply access Creator Studio and select the following:

- Video Manager
- Select the video you'd like to add the card to
- Next, select the "I" icon to access the cards page
- Add a card to your video by clicking "add card"

Next, simply click on the type of card you'd like to add. You'll be asked to add a bit of text to your card. This is the text that shows up in your video at the set time.

How Should You Use Cards?

Anytime I mention a related video that viewers might want to check out, I add a card. Anytime I do a collaboration with another YouTuber, I use the card to add a clickable link to their channel. You can also use cards to link out to a website, which makes list building a piece of cake on YouTube.

YouTube End Screen

The YouTube end screen also makes it easy to add clickable functionality to a video. Cards are powerful because they can be added anywhere into a video; however, the drawback of a card is that they're small and inconspicuous.

The YouTube end screen, however, makes it possible to add large clickable elements within the last twenty seconds of a video, hence the name, "end screen."

End screens come with a few limitations. As mentioned, an end screen element can only be added to the last twenty seconds of a video. I haven't found this to be an issue. It's plenty of time to create my call to action.

If you add a YouTube end screen, at least one of the elements must be either another YouTube video or playlist. YouTube does this because their goal, as I keep saying, is to keep viewers watching longer.

You can see an example of my end screen on the next few pages. You can see that I've created a simple "less is more" end screen template. Note: The video in the upper righthand corner, the words "Subscribe & Feed a Poodle," and the picture of me and my poodles were added via editing prior to uploading the template to YouTube. The first image below shows the end screen template without the YouTube functionality in place. Now, time to add the bells and whistles. I can add links to additional videos, links to my associated website, another YouTuber's channel, and more. Yet again, creating a simple system makes it easy for me to move forward.

The second image shows the end screen after adding the various elements provided by YouTube's end screen functionality.

Blank End Screen Template I Created

End Screen with YouTube Functionality Added

Convert More Views!

Convert More Viewers into
Subscribers with my FREE
Custom End Screen Templates
Packaged with My YouTube
Starter Kit! You Dig?

Access: BrianGJohnson.TV/Free

CHAPTER SEVEN

Playlist Ritual Phase Two

In Chapter Four, we covered phase one of the Playlist Ritual—how you can leverage playlists to create an engaging channel experience that results in viewers watching more of your videos. This leads to greater watch time and can help you achieve authority faster. After all, viewers watching multiple videos from your channel sends a clear signal to YouTube that you have an *engaging channel* that viewers enjoy, the very thing that YouTube rewards.

Ritual Playlist Optimization

Earlier, I also introduced you to the concept of focusing on your channel overall rather than ranking individual videos. And we went into depth on how you can leverage thumbnails combined with playlists to create a congruent experience that results in additional views.

In this chapter, we're going to focus on phase two of the Playlist Ritual: how you can manage, tweak, and optimize a playlist *over time* to drive even more views. Allow me to mention an obvious fact: The more videos you publish, the better your results will be. Can I get an amen (or a duh)?

This doesn't mean that you need to publish an insane number of videos forever. It's quite the opposite. After you've gained momentum and authority, your videos will continue to rank, drive views, and convert viewers into subscribers. Check out the stats below from my channel.

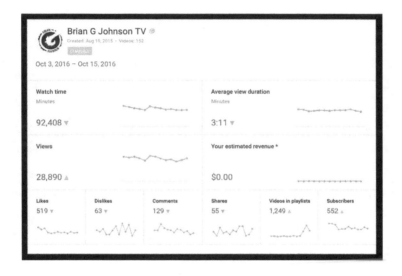

The screenshot shows that from October 3 to October 15, 2016, my channel drove 28,000-plus video views and gained 552 subscribers. During this time, I didn't upload a single video yet my channel continued to grow. Once your channel gains authority, YouTube itself creates tremendous momentum that will carry on and build your channel over time. So, when life gets in the way of making videos, it's okay. Your channel and subscribers will be there when you return. Of course, if you break for an extremely long period, well that's another story.

To drive these kinds of results, you must gain **authority** and publish ranking videos. Most YouTubers are never able to do that because their videos are *not engaging* compared to what's currently ranking on

YouTube. Or they never took the time to select the *right keywords* to target. Or they gave up before the magic happens—this is the fate for so many. Their goals and/or wants are simply unrealistic. They are unable to generate results quickly, so they quit. Sad but true. It boils down to those two things: video engagement and keyword selection.

In Chapter Eight, I'll cover keyword selection in-depth. I'll also make available to you free video training on this very subject.

The bottom line is this: it takes great effort to publish engaging videos. Most YouTubers with large subscriber bases have been publishing videos consistently for years. Over time, their videos got better and more engaging. They got more comfortable in front of the camera, their editing skills improved, their ability to create a thumbnail that entices a click improved, and so on.

This, by the way, is why a Tube Ritual 30-Day Challenge is so very powerful. It focuses on engagement as well as keyword selection. It forces you to work hard to ensure you're able to increase your results exponentially. Most thirty-day challenges that I've been associated with focus primarily on getting comfortable in front of the camera and creating videos. If that's where you're at, wonderful! I'm excited for you and what lies ahead in your video creation journey.

However, if you're going to take the time to create videos, why not create videos that are optimized to rank and drive views? After all, isn't that why you're on YouTube in the first place; to not only share your message but to amplify it and inspire people to act?

As you move forward with your Tube Ritual 30-Day Challenge, note that it makes the most sense to focus on publishing videos into one or two playlists rather than publishing videos into a bunch of playlists.

Why? Because we want our videos to appear together in search results and in Suggested Videos. And this is more likely to happen as you publish more and more videos into a single playlist.

Common Suggested Video Ranking Factors

There are several tactics you can use to help more of your videos show up in Suggested Videos. These include:

- **Channel Tag Tactic**
  Create a common *channel tag* that you enter into the YouTube tag section for each video you upload. Using one tag across all your uploaded videos helps YouTube identify the correlation.
- **Official Playlist Tactic**
  Create a playlist, then click "official" playlist button.

Make no mistake, a myriad of factors determine which videos show up in Suggested Videos and getting yours there isn't easy (depending on the search term and density of results).

The more weight, ranking power, and authority other Suggested Videos have, the more authority, ranking power, and weight your video will need to show up among them. For example, if a video is driving five hundred video views a day, that's a lot of authority and juice. To show up with that video in search or Suggested, then your video must also have similar authority and juice.

As mentioned earlier, my primary source of views come from Suggested Videos. During the summer of 2016, about a month after wrapping up a thirty-day challenge and tweaking some of my playlists based on what I'm sharing with you, Suggested Videos overtook my search referrals.

During this time, I noticed that I was dominating my own videos in Suggested, meaning most videos showing up in the Suggested section on my own videos were my other videos. At the time, each of my playlists had a few winners that were ranking well in search and driving views.

Since I was dominating my own video pages, those winning videos were pushing views to my other videos in the respected playlist.

In time, those videos began to rank better and my winners began to show up on other people's video pages as they were accumulating serious watch time. The result was even more views for the winners, as well as all the videos in the playlist.

Coming to YouTube with many years of Google SEO experience under my belt, my focus for getting ranked was on YouTube search. I never realized how many views Suggested Videos can drive.

For example, a given search term may drive a total of 1,000 daily views. These views are split across the first twenty or so videos that rank for the given search term. Thus, only a small percentage of published videos have a chance to rank and drive traffic for the given term.

Those videos that are ranking are driving consistent views day in and day out. Each day, as they drive more and more views, they gain more and more accumulated watch time. As a result, they get more and more authoritative.

As a video gains more authority, it's more likely to rank well in search and show up in Suggested Videos. This is where things get exciting.

Often there are hundreds of thousands of videos that have been published on a given topic. One way to identify just how many videos have been published on a topic is to pay attention to the search results for a given keyword phrase.

In the image on the next page, I've searched for "Apple branding." Notice that 175,000 YouTube search results appear. That's a staggering number of results.

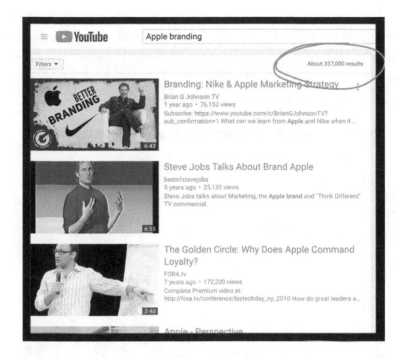

There are a couple of things worth noting here. Number one, I'm number one in search. Number two, the video is seven months old. Number three, other videos appearing for this search term are two and six years old. Imagine publishing a video that drives views, subscribers, leads, and traffic for years. That's the power of YouTube.

Back to our Suggested Video strategy. If 175,000 videos show up for "Apple branding," then I would imagine that means my video could potentially show in Suggested Videos on hundreds of thousands of related video pages.

That's a lot of video pages to show up on, and while my video most likely does not show up on 175,000 video pages, I'm sure it shows up on some. The number one traffic source (73 percent) is Suggested Videos, views coming primarily from other people's video pages.

The potential to drive crazy views is enormous with Suggested Videos. Dominate your own videos in Suggested, and you'll increase your accumulated watch time and create a sticky channel for viewers, which in turn sends a signal to YouTube (this is an engaging channel), which of course can lead to even more authority.

Additional Suggested Video Ranking Factors

I previously mentioned the more common Suggested Video tactics, including using a channel tag, as well as making sure that you're creating "official" playlists. Next, I'll cover other factors that you can leverage (some more than others) to improve the likelihood that you'll show up in Suggested Videos.

As I wrote out this list, it became obvious that these items fall into one of two categories: **Relevancy** or **Engagement**. Make no mistake, nothing is more important than these two elements when it comes to increasing video engagement overall. That's why this book began with engagement.

Video Title Relevancy

Videos that contain the keywords in the title have increased odds of showing up in Suggested Videos. This is an easy win, especially when crafting your own playlists. For example, my "iMovie" playlist always contains that word and usually also contains the following: iPhone, iPad, iOS.

Accumulated Watch Time

This is a biggie. Accumulated watch time is a simple way for YouTube to gauge overall video authority. As a video gains more and more views, accumulated watch time increases, and the likelihood of the video showing up in Suggested increases as well.

Overall Channel Authority

I believe YouTube wants to identify not just engaging videos, but rather engaging channels, because an engaging channel will draw a user back to the YouTube website again and again. A single engaging video, however, won't do that after it's been viewed one or two times. Thus, I think YouTube likely measures a channel's overall authority, and that authority may be applied to the Suggested Video algorithm. How can you improve your channel authority? Simple, follow this guide to creating playlists that increase the number of video views your channel drives upon discovery.

Publishing Frequency

When I participated in my own thirty-day challenge, my authority increased substantially. One reason why this might have happened is based on a YouTube metric called "Session Time." Session time is another way for YouTube to measure the authority of a channel versus a single video. Anytime a YouTube viewer accesses YouTube and begins watching videos, a new session is created. The first video the user watches is credited with the "session." Thus, if a user accesses the site, then clicks on your video, you're credited with the session. If you're uploading often, that would increase the likelihood that subscribers would be starting sessions by clicking on one of your videos, because your videos would be showing up in the subscriber feed, on the homepage, and more. Just one more reason why a thirty-day challenge can be so incredibly powerful. That was certainly the case for me.

Meta Tags

Meta tags most likely play a role in the Suggested Video algorithm. Without question, this is something to pay attention to. However, I think far too many YouTubers place too much weight on meta tags. I believe ranking factors that measure user engagement are much more important, therefore simply using all the right meta tags does not equal ranking. Watch time, average view duration, or audience retention are far more important.

Relative Audience Retention & Average View Duration

As mentioned in the previous paragraph, this is what I focus on because I believe it powers YouTube discoverability.

Level of Engagement

Another easy way for YouTube to gauge whether viewers like a video would be to simply measure the level of engagement beyond watch time and duration. This could easily be done by measuring video likes, comments, shares, and you can return to the video to watch it again.

Viewer to Subscriber Ratio

Like level of engagement, YouTube could easily measure the percentage of nonsubscribers who subscribe to a channel via the video view page or after accessing a channel page. Again, this would be simple for YouTube to measure providing insight into whether viewers "like" a video.

YouTube has access to a crazy amount of viewer data that it can and does use to decide which videos show up as Suggested. Nobody knows exactly how the YouTube algorithm is powered; however, I do know that these elements I've just mentioned can and will help you overall on YouTube.

I think my own results in search and Suggested Videos speak for themselves. Focus on creating very niche specific playlists, and you can greatly improve your ability to drive more views.

I began my channel with one playlist for "apps" and later separated that one playlist into three:

- iMovie (Mobile Editing)
- Apps for Editing
- Apps for Photo Editing

Creating very niche specific playlists makes it easy for YouTube to understand that these videos are part of a group. It's led to these videos showing up more often in Suggested and gives the viewer more viewing options.

Another great example of this is my playlist for custom thumbnails. I don't think I've ever seen a similar channel with a playlist just for thumbnails; however, the result is that more of my thumbnail videos get in front of viewers searching for this very subject. It's a win/win for everyone, including me.

I spend a fair amount of time tending to my channel and playlists. I tweak thumbnail concepts (colors, fonts, style) and organize my playlists and their placement on my channel to ensure I can drive more views to specific videos.

The goal, as always, is to increase views, rank higher in search, and gain more subscribers. Tweaking, optimizing, and maximizing is what the phase two of the Playlist Ritual is all about.

This is something I usually do after I wrap up a thirty-day challenge and here's why: Nothing is more powerful than uploading more videos. I know it's obvious, but it bears mentioning again in case you missed it the first two hundred times I said it. If uploading another video is more important than tweaking existing videos, then I focus on a very simple plan of action during my challenge.

Priority One During a Challenge-Uploading

1. I focus on one or two of my playlists (especially if my playlists only have a few videos)
2. Create videos
3. Identify the target keyword phrase for each video
4. Craft a thumbnail for the said video
5. Publish
6. Write the title, tags, and video description
7. Add cards and end screens
8. Email my list
9. Post to social media (video link)
10. Think about what I'll create tomorrow

That's a solid half day of work, and I know with each new upload I'm doing the most important and powerful things when it comes to driving results. This is all I worry about when I'm in the middle of a Tube Ritual

Challenge. Afterward, I may come back to tweak a playlist by organizing the video order or sometimes even testing out a new thumbnail look.

The moral of the story is this: During a challenge, I keep things as **simple as possible**. Later, when I have more time to ponder, I may tweak and improve my channel and playlists (if needed). Sometimes there are exceptions, where I'll tweak something during a challenge, but most often I keep things simple and that makes it easier for me to focus on my next upload.

You dig? Good!

Playlist & Channel Optimization

We've proven that it's easier to drive more views by focusing and building out playlists rather than publishing individual videos. However, there's more good news. How you structure a playlist can greatly increase views across your channel.

In fact, how you structure your playlists and how you integrate those playlists on your channel impacts views substantially.

But wait, there's more! It's also possible to improve your subscriber growth rate by structuring your playlist based on which videos convert more viewers into subscribers and by how you integrate each playlist in your channel design.

Before we dive into the details of how to make this work, it's important to first set some rules of the road.

YouTube & Suggested Videos

First off, it's highly unlikely that you'll be able to take up the entire Suggested Video section no matter how well optimized and/or engaging your videos are.

I personally believe that YouTube organizes Suggested Videos with a couple of things in mind. Number one, variety is the spice of life, and to that end, YouTube wants to list a variety of videos for viewers to select and watch.

Second, YouTube wants to promote channels that show engagement. YouTube wants to see channels succeed because the more channels that are succeeding, the stronger YouTube is overall. This is neither a good thing or a bad thing. It just is.

It's impossible for you to own 100 percent of your Suggested Videos, that means that it is possible for you to show up on someone else's video page. That's a good thing. Last, most YouTubers don't take the time to do what I'm teaching you to do, or you'll win in the long run because you'll dominate your Suggested Videos and in time, you will show up on other people's pages. That's a win!

Suggested Video Topics & Authoritative Videos

Earlier, I mentioned that without question, relevancy is something that I believe has an impact on the Suggested Video algorithm. However, as I've studied the algorithm, it's become clear to me that authority plays a far greater role when it comes to showing up on other people's video pages.

This is especially true when showing up on other people's video pages that carry a lot of authority or are driving a lot of views.

Video Page Example

The above screen capture highlights one of my video pages (it features one of my videos from my channel). The video featured is one of my most authoritative videos, and it drives hundreds of daily views.

How YouTube Measures Authority

What I'm about to share with you is my personal belief and viewpoint. I don't have any hard data to back it up; however, I'm confident in this concept of authority. I feel fine sharing it with you.

The Big Idea

Videos gain authority on YouTube in a variety of ways. Videos that gain above-average authority begin to rank in YouTube search and are heavily promoted in Suggested Videos.

Authority is measured in many ways, so one video may rank well based on its incredibly high relative audience retention (RAR) metrics, while another video may have slightly above-average RAR, but has accumulated a lot of watch time.

Above average is a sliding scale based on the authority of other videos that are ranking for a given search query or showing up for a specific topic in Suggested Videos.

For example, to publish a video that ranks well in search and shows up in Suggested Videos on the topic of "iMovie effects," the video needs to gain enough authority to outpace videos that are currently ranking for the given search query.

Let's look at the YouTube ranking metrics:

- Keyword Relevancy
- Accumulated Watch Time
- Relative Audience Retention

Factor One: Keyword Phrase Relevancy

Once you understand the concept of keyword relevancy, it's far easier to identify which keyword phrases it makes sense to target. Numerous factors can and do impact scoring when it comes to relevancy alone. In this example, let's look at the following keyword phrase: *iMovie App Tutorial.*

Search Query: iMovie App Tutorial

This is a three-word query. It's important to note that video titles that contain more than three words become less and less relevant. For example, the four-word video title *iMovie App Tutorial iPhone* is more relevant than the six-word video title *iMovie App Tutorial iPhone iPad iOS.*

This is one of the thousands of examples of how relevancy works. Another factor to consider when studying keyword relevancy is the prominence of the keyword. Prominence simply means how soon does the search query come in the title.

In this video title example, *iMovie App Tutorial iPhone* is more relevant than *iPhone iMovie App Tutorial* because the search query comes first.

SIDE NOTE: It's far easier to rank in search if you publish a video that is optimized for a 100 percent relevancy scoring. The process is simple, and in our example of *iMovie App Tutorial*, you would add that phrase (and only that phrase) to the video title. You would begin the video description with the phrase, and you would write a series of meta tags around this phrase. By the way, this is how I ranked my *iMovie Tutorial* video when I first published it. Because I had a 100 percent relevancy score, I had an easier time competing with other videos that were already ranking for this phrase.

Furthermore, out of the ranking videos that were not as optimized and in the first ten video positions, only a few videos contained the three words mentioned in their video title.

However, the other videos ranked well because of other factors that may have included accumulated watch time and or relative audience retention.

Again, these three metrics are:

- Keyword Relevancy
- Accumulated Watch Time
- Relative Audience Retention

I believe each metric carries great influence on the algorithm. The first two can result in amazing rankings for videos within hours of publishing, even for channels with zero subscribers, because these factors are not measuring "how many people" but rather:

- **Relevancy:** How closely does the video title and topic match that of the search query?
- **Relative Audience Retention:** How well did viewers like this video in comparison to that of videos of a similar topic?

Paying attention to what people are searching for and just how well current ranking videos are optimized for relevancy makes it far easier for those who are just getting started on the platform to publish videos that drive consistent views.

Factor Two: Accumulated Watch Time

Accumulated watch time is just the opposite. It rewards volume, i.e., more minutes watched with more authority, which can lead to better search rankings.

For example, a video with a total of 1,000 minutes watched is more authoritative than a video with a total of 100 minutes watched. However, if the video with only 100 minutes of accumulated watch time has a higher relevancy score, it may outrank the video with 1,000 minutes of accumulative minutes watched.

SIDE NOTE: If you're struggling to rank videos, simply identify an exact search query in YouTube and use that for the video title, the beginning of the video description, and write a handful of meta tags around this one phase. Later, if a video is driving consistent views, then it's also accumulating watch time and you may want to add a few additional keyword phrases to the video title.

This strategy has served me well. after a video drives 500 to 1,000 views, I will add a few more keywords to the title. If the video was ranking for the first primary keyword I targeted and it does not drop in the search rankings, then I wait for another 500 to 1,000 views and add a few more keywords to the title once again.

This works because early on, a video ranks based on its relevancy. Later, it ranks for its accumulated watch time and relevancy; however, the relevancy score drops a bit as you add more keyword phrases.

Factor Three: Relative Audience Retention

Again, in my humble opinion, the most important ranking factor to YouTube is *engagement*. The easiest way for you to measure engagement on a per video basis is to pay attention to relative audience retention.

I've seen videos with high relative audience retention scores rank incredibly well in YouTube. Even better, I've seen YouTube promote videos within hours of publication, meaning that you don't have to have a ton of views, and you don't have to have a ton of accumulated watch time if a video has a very high audience retention score.

This information is based on my experience with my videos. However, I've also heard other YouTube experts mention similar results, so I believe the theory is valid.

Nothing is more important than engagement (yes, I'll keep saying it!) and while many struggling YouTubers may disagree, I believe engagement is more important (to YouTube) than the number of subscribers you might have.

Again, this is how I believe YouTube measures authority:

- Keyword Relevancy
- Accumulated Watch Time
- Relative Audience Retention

Focus on these three elements and you will publish videos that rank high in YouTube search, which can drive consistent views and greater accumulated watch time.

My Best Performing Videos

I wanted to share the following information so you have an idea of what you might expect if you follow my ritual. In my experience, I've seen my best-performing videos begin to rank in YouTube search. Over time, these videos increased in search rankings and drove even more views. After a while, these videos began to show up as Suggested Videos. Once videos gain this momentum, views can go through the roof based on the potential of Suggested Videos.

sOpportunity: Playlist Organization & Optimization

As you can see, many factors lead to determining what types of videos will rank high in search and ultimately drive views on a consistent basis.

Earlier I talked about the power of creating very niche based playlists that cover very specific topics. This is powerful because it can help you show up more often in Suggested Videos and lead to more views.

Now I want to share with you a few tips on organizing a playlist and the impact it can have on channel growth.

Authority Trumps All

When I look at Suggested Videos, I often see that there's not a huge correlation in the relevancy of keyword queries. Earlier, I mentioned that it's helpful to target similar keyword phrases in your video titles, and I stand by that. I do believe that it is part of the algorithm and can help to ensure that more of your videos show up on your video pages.

However, when it comes to showing up on other people's video pages, **authority trumps all** (accumulated minutes watched). It would also seem that YouTube is less concerned with the relevancy of video titles and instead cherry picks videos that are based on a similar subject.

In the screen capture below, notice video #3 and video #4. Both contain the word "iMovie" and "iPhone and iPad." Thus, the video titles do not score in relevancy, but they are based on the same subject matter as the video featured on the page, which is about editing with iMovie for iPhone/iPad.

Last, notice that video #3 only has 2,000 views. My guess is that those 2,000 views resulted in a high retention score and that's why it's listed on my video page.

I know the horse I'm beating has been long dead, but engagement is king.

Video Page Example

The more popular a subject is on YouTube, the more potential views there are to drive to it. In the example above, the topic of "iMovie Effects" is pretty popular. I am targeting a phrase that is not impossible to rank for in search, however, it's competitive. Likewise, videos that drive lots of views are hard to show up on, it's competitive and you must beat out other videos to show up there.

Also, note, that the order in which you list the videos within a playlist can impact the order in which videos show up on your Suggested Video pages. The order is also important when you add a playlist to your channel page. The best strategy is to list your most authoritative videos first in a playlist and your weakest videos last.

Doing this results in more views for those videos, which increases accumulated watch time and may help those videos show up on other people's video pages over time.

For example, if you have a YouTube playlist that has twenty or more videos, the first five videos in that playlist are displayed on your channel page and viewed more often simply because of their position on the page.

Check out the screenshot below. Notice my channel page features my "SEO for YouTube" playlist. The first video in the playlist is "How to Increase Your YouTube Views, Channel Authority." This video is ranking well, driving views, and I positioned it first within the playlist to drive even more views to increase the search rankings as quickly as possible.

The second video is my "YouTube Keyword Tool" video. This is another video that is ranking well, has great retention, and is also converting viewers into subscribers.

Playlist Optimization: Viewer to Subscriber Ratio

That last sentence was important. That video is doing a good job at *converting viewers into subscribers*. I organize my videos based on how they're ranking in search, the potential number of views in the future, and how well they're converting viewers into subscribers.

A video may be ranking and driving views, however, if it's not converting, then you may want to position that video lower in the playlist. After you've finished up your **Tube Ritual 30-Day Challenge**, you may want to tweak your playlist based on these factors.

The point of this is to keep in mind the part playlists play when it comes to the ranking factors in the YouTube algorithm. This information will serve you well as you dive into the next chapter where we lay out our plan of attack for your thirty-day challenge. Fasten your seatbelts, because the ride is about to begin.

CHAPTER EIGHT

Tube Ritual 30-Day Challenge

The Power & Momentum of One More Video

Nothing impacts channel growth more than the consistent publishing of videos filled with great content that keeps your audience coming back for more. I'm not talking about releasing a video here and a video there whenever you feel like it. I'm talking about consistently releasing a steady stream of videos, preferably every day or two. That's the key to real channel growth.

Engagement with the viewer is also a vital part of growing your channel, so the more engaging your content (entertaining, informative, educational, etc.), the greater chance you will have of connecting with your audience to build loyalty and viewership.

As you move forward with your own personal thirty-day challenge, focus on improving engagement with every video you upload.

Also, keep in mind that forcing yourself to publish new videos on a set schedule will help you create systems that make the process easier and more efficient. It's been said that if you do something consistently for twenty-one days, it becomes a habit. Make a habit of consistently publishing great video content.

The more videos you publish, the better you will get at every aspect of the process. You will learn to simplify the process and hone the workflow so you can more easily publish another video tomorrow and the next day and the next.

Don't expect your channel to catch fire right out of the gate. Creating more engaging videos is a process that is learned and improved upon over time. That's why many channels seem to flatline at the beginning, then start to build a steady base of subscribers over time.

Building a successful YouTube channel takes time, testing, and persistence. Remember this adage: If it was easy, everyone would do it. Tell yourself that whenever you feel that building your YouTube channel takes too much time and effort. Successful channel creators also take the time to learn what works and what doesn't and improve upon their content and processes along the way.

For example, over time you'll become more comfortable in front of the camera and begin to improve on the style of videos that you create. Many creators find that their style and on-camera persona change over time as they get more comfortable being in front of a camera and learn what's truly important to their audience. Chances are yours will too. Your skills and abilities will naturally improve because you're creating more videos, which will positively impact your engagement level.

In his book *Outliers*, author Malcolm Gladwell theorized that you could master any skill if you did it for 10,000 hours.

While I don't think that it'll take you that long to build a successful YouTube channel, the logic behind his theory is sound. The more you do something, the better you get at it and the easier it becomes to do. It usually takes a while for a video to gain traction on YouTube and show up in the search results. I have seen videos that had exceptionally high relative audience retention rank quickly in YouTube search, and that usually happens for a number of reasons. Most notably because YouTube rewards "engaging video that keeps viewers watching." High relative audience retention is a metric that measures "how long viewers are watching."

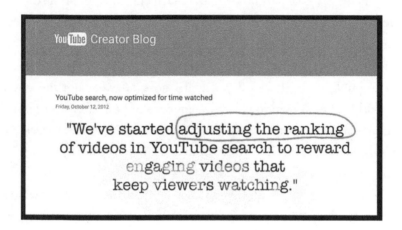

However, if you're targeting search terms that are more evergreen (long-lasting) in nature or search terms that have a fair amount of competition, it may take upwards of three to twelve weeks for a video to rank high in search, if it ranks high at all. Some videos just need more time to rise in rankings. They need more "accumulated watch time." I've seen many videos that didn't initially do well in the search results increase in search rankings after thirty days or more. One of my best performing videos generated just a handful of daily views over a four-month period, then began to show up higher in YouTube search, which generated fifty to two hundred views a day.

After several weeks, the same video began to show up in Suggested Videos. So, time can be your friend when it comes to seeing your video rise in the search results. As you move forward in your journey and start publishing more videos, pay close attention to your videos' rankings, but don't get disheartened if a video isn't immediately high in search. I know that it's hard not to get discouraged, however, also remember that it's possible to see rankings improve after several weeks.

Your Tube Ritual Challenge Goal

Whenever I take part in a YouTube challenge, i.e., publish so many videos in so many days, I set my goals with flexibility and the end result in mind.

For example, if it's a "thirty videos in thirty days" challenge, I do my best to publish one video a day, but if I miss a day, it's not the end of the world. Also, as mentioned, the frequency of how often you publish is totally up to you. I recommend a minimum of three videos weekly to see substantial growth. However, that recommendation is just that—a recommendation.

If my goal is to publish thirty videos in thirty days—not one video per day—it doesn't matter to me if I publish one video every day or two videos every other day, so long as thirty videos are published within thirty days. Life sometimes gets in the way. If I miss a day, that's okay because it's the end goal that's important (thirty videos in thirty days), not the schedule on which I publish them.

The point of a challenge like this is to get you to publish more videos, because the more videos you publish, the better you will become at every step of the process, and the better your result will be, i.e., higher rankings, more watch time, more subscribers, longer engagement, etc.

By the time you've published thirty videos in thirty days, your on-camera comfort level, the style in which you present, your production skills and overall processes should be exponentially better than they were just thirty days ago.

You should also be much more skilled at selecting keywords that draw an audience to you, creating great thumbnails that catch the viewer's eye and writing descriptions that get you ranked highly in search.

It's been said that there is great power in writing down your goals and making them as specific as possible. Just keep in mind that even written goals are not set in stone.

For example, if you're interested in participating in *Vlog Every Day* (April/August), also known as VEDA, but the idea of publishing a video every day is simply overwhelming to you, I suggest that you take on the challenge, but set your own weekly goals rather than adhere to the daily goals suggested by the challenge.

Rather than publishing a vlog every day, publish three or four videos a week during the challenge. You get bonus points if you announce your intention to the world. Again, keep in mind the real reason you would participate in such a challenge. It's not to prove that you can publish a video a day, though you should certainly try if possible. It's to prove to yourself that you can consistently publish great content on a regular schedule over the course of the month.

If you hit thirty videos in thirty days, kudos to you! But if you only publish twenty-five videos, don't beat yourself up, so long as you've honed your craft and improved your video quality and processes along the way.

Simple (Optimized for YouTube) Videos

If your goal is to publish more videos more often and increase your skill level by doing so, then you can greatly increase your chances of reaching your goals by creating what I call "simple videos." I believe this is the best strategy for anyone just starting out on YouTube. Often, new YouTube creators will see videos with high-production values, shot with expensive cameras, microphones, and drones, and think they must start at that level right out of the gate to compete and succeed.

The truth is, most of those videos are created by people with far more time, money, and experience than the average YouTube newcomer. Most of them started out doing simple videos, and you should too.

Keep It Simple Stupid (KISS)

A simple video is just that: a simple, barebones video without all the special effects, swirling graphics, flying text, or other whiz-bang elements you may see other video producers using (sometimes using them badly).

If you're just getting started, do yourself a huge favor and keep the process as simple as possible in the beginning, then add varying degrees of complexity over time as your skills increase.

A simple video is one that you can quickly and easily create using the knowledge, skills, equipment, and talents that you already possess.

For example, the simplest of simple videos might require no greater learning curve than knowing how to turn on your webcam and upload the video to YouTube.

A simple video could be you talking to your webcam, or talking over a PowerPoint or narrating a video. Or using your phone to record a presentation or a daily vlog as you walk around the park.

The key is to keep things simple: simple to conceptualize, simple to create, simple to produce, and simple to publish to YouTube. Start simple, publish a bunch of videos, then start adding other elements that you feel will add value to your videos. Over time, you'll greatly improve your skillset while maintaining the ability to create and publish videos on a consistent basis. That' the very thing that the YouTube algorithm rewards, frequent uploads.

In the past, I've focused on learning the skills required to accomplish a task ahead of time, so those skills are in my bag of tricks even before I need them. For example, back in 2002 when I was first learning about Google's search engine optimization strategies, I launched a website that focused on cooking. I had worked for years as a chef, so it was a subject I knew well, and it would be easy for me to create great content for such a site. It would also be a good way for me to gain the knowledge and skills required to drive traffic to a website that featured a topic I knew well.

Once I learned how to drive thousands of views and tons of visitors a day to my cooking site, I took the knowledge of SEO I had gained, and the skills I had developed, and put them to work on more profitable subject matters.

Learning and honing those skills ahead of time on my cooking site made it easier for me to drive customers to my "money sites" later on, because I had taken the time to learn the skills that were needed in order to achieve the results I was after. So many YouTubers focus on the money or the subscribers first. Without the right skillsets, generating results is nearly impossible. This is why so many people struggle to succeed on YouTube.

When I launched my new YouTube channel, Brian G Johnson TV, my initial goal was to gain the skills and abilities that would allow me to create cool looking videos that would generate lots of views down the road. Once I obtained those basic skills, I then put them into play and focused more on getting higher rankings, more views, and more subscribers.

The lesson is this: take the time to learn and hone the skills required to just get started on YouTube, put those skills into practice, then learn and hone the next set of skills that will take you to the next level.

There is no magic pill. You can't hire someone to build your YouTube empire for you. Lots of people try to shortcut the process. They spend tons of money on apps and virtual assistants and "how to get rich on YouTube" programs and goofy "too good to be true software." Learn, practice, improve, rinse and repeat.

The Importance of *YouTube* Optimized Videos

While I firmly believe in the power of simplicity, be careful not to oversimplify the process. Statistically speaking, the videos that drive the best results on YouTube do so because the topic they address is popular or trending, the keywords have been thoroughly researched and refined, and the video content is geared toward a specific topic or audience.

Many video creators have oversimplified the process to the point of being ineffective. They pull out their phone and create a live video on Facebook, Periscope, or for any of the emerging platforms, and then publish that video over to YouTube without giving thought to things like relevancy and keywords. These videos almost always do not contain a YouTube specific call to action, such as subscribe and the results are almost always the same. These videos don't drive views, rarely convert viewers into subscribers, and may even hurt an overall channel.

Keep in mind the importance of structure. Most high-performing YouTube videos have a beginning, a middle, and an end. Most of the time they also include calls to action specific to YouTube that live videos cannot incorporate. And last, live video is typically not as polished as high-ranking YouTube video content. As I write this, YouTube Live is currently rolling out to channels with 10,000 subscribers. This will be a game changer without question. However, make no mistake, those who will win with YouTube Live will be those who create live streams that are optimized for YouTube. I believe live video is a powerful form of media, and I use it alongside YouTube to build my brand and amplify my message. As you move forward and create videos optimized specifically for YouTube, remember to incorporate the following calls to action that help engage the audience and turn them into subscribers:

- Tell the viewer to subscribe within the first minute (hit that subscribe button!).
- Tell the viewer to subscribe again at the end of the video.
- Include other calls to action at the end of the video (visit my website, find me on Facebook, check out my book, etc.).

CHAPTER NINE

Tube Rank Ritual 12-Step Program

"Hello, my name is Brian. I'm a YouTube-aholic. In the past few months, I've uploaded forty-nine videos. I need help."

Now that you have an idea of how I approach the creation of my own videos and how I get them ranked highly in YouTube search, I'm going to take you by the hand and guide you through this challenge.

I'm going to share with you how I personally create videos, identify trending topics, target keyword phrases, and upload videos to YouTube. I'll also cover what I think you should focus on most to improve engagement and watch time.

The Importance of Research

The first step in your journey is learning how to research topics and keyword phrases so you can identify the best phrases to target that will get you higher rankings and more views.

Remember, it's not the phrase with the most search volume that you want to target. Rather, it's the keyword phrase that will help your video rank higher in search and thus drive more views.

Identify the *Right* Keyword Phrase

Identifying the right keyword phrase to target can make or break a channel, regardless of how good the content might be.

Many YouTube creators fail to identify and implement the actual keyword phrases that people are searching for. As a result, they never see their rankings and views grow.

Some creators simply don't understand or realize the importance of using keywords to drive views and give little thought to the titles and descriptions of their videos.

Others, such as daily vloggers, think they can't target keyword phrases because their videos are based on daily activities. This is a misguided way of thinking because no matter what kind of videos you create, you can—and should—associate the video to keyword phrases that will get you higher in ranking.

For example, if you're a vlogger and you create a video that features you preparing chicken piccata, you can include the phrase "chicken piccata" in the title of the video.

Your vlog may not be about food; however, if your video is engaging (the most critical element for success), viewers who found your video through the search term "chicken piccata" may still subscribe to your channel.

Some creators who claim to do effective keyword research may not be doing so using the strategies covered here. Rather, they hastily select phrases based on what they first encounter or phrases that contain the most search volume. That's a huge mistake.

When I launched my new channel on YouTube in March 2016, I made this mistake. I published a video targeting the keyword phrase "how to get more views on YouTube." This phrase had 91 million search results on YouTube. I thought, *Wow, that's a great phrase to target!*

Now, remember those three important YouTube ranking factors discussed earlier: accumulated watch time, relative audience retention, and keyword relevancy.

The top ten ranking videos for this search phrase belonged to YouTubers with lots of subscribers, something I neglected to think about when doing my research.

Subscribers to a channel typically watch videos longer than nonsubscribers, so when creators with lots of active subscribers publish videos, they typically have longer watch times, which can affect ranking. Furthermore, these videos also have above average audience retention metrics because, again, subscribers watch longer.

Lots of subscribers can also result in higher view counts, which means the accumulated minutes watched push the video higher in the rankings. Finally, most of the top videos were highly optimized for keyword relevancy. The bottom line was, this was a super-competitive and challenging keyword phrase to rank for, a lesson I learned the hard way. The lesson I learned from trying to target such a high-volume search phrase was this: It makes far more sense to target keyword phrases that drive far less volume but offer a better shot at landing high in the search ranking and to leverage the power of relevancy.

If you can't get a video into the top twenty or so videos for a specific search phrase, it doesn't matter how much search volume the phrase is driving. It's like trying to merge onto a busy highway with millions of cars going 100 miles an hour and you're in a go-cart. You're going to get run over and left dazed and confused on the side of the road. There is no other possible outcome.

I took a step back, realized the mistakes and the assumptions I'd made, then implemented the keyword research strategies I'd previously learned to identify phrases that would give me a chance to rank high in search.

For example, if you search for "Increase Your YouTube Views" you'll find one or two of my videos ranking in the top ten. This search phrase does not drive a ton of views; however, it does drive some views and my video is getting a fair share of those views. Furthermore, my video is converting viewers into subscribers. That's a win in my book and even better. Every day my channel grows a bit stronger as I gain more active subscribers. In time, I will hit a tipping point. That happened for my buddy Nick Nimmin and as I finish editing this book, it's now happening to me. It all begins by targeting one specific keyword phrase.

The Primary Keyword Phrase

One important thing to understand about YouTube is that it's a search engine. Most viewers enter search terms or phrases into the search box to quickly locate videos that interest them. The more relevant a video's title is, the greater its chances of showing up in the search results.

That's why it's best to target one search query with each video you publish and to create a video title that is highly relevant to the query. I often create video titles that are 100 percent relevant. For example, one of my videos targets the search query "YouTube Keyword Tool." My video title is "YouTube Keyword Tool," so this video gets a 100 percent relevancy score.

One rule to remember is this: The more competitive the search phrase, the higher you want your relevancy score to be.

As your channel grows and you're able to drive more and more views within the first seventy-two hours of publishing, you may want to start including additional keyword phrases so you show up for more than one keyword search because your video will rank based on accumulated watch time and audience retention.

For example, people find my iMovie video for hundreds of different keyword phrases. Two of which are:

- How to Use iMovie
- iMovie App Tutorial

My video title contains both phrases as well as additional phrases because it's very authoritative, meaning that it now has a high relative audience retention score as well as accumulated watch time.

It also contains lots of keyword phrases in the video title. Combined, these elements help the video rank for a number of phrases and it's driven over 29,000 views in its first six months.

The strategy is simple. If your channel is new or you're struggling to drive views, choose one search query and use that exact phrase as your video title and nothing else. Again! **Only add one exact YouTube keyword phrase to your video title.**

Tube Ritual Search Opportunity

You don't have to spend a ton of time researching keyword phrases to identify how competitive they are. In fact, here's how I do it, quickly and easily.

YouTube "authority" is measured by the following metrics:

- Relative Audience Retention
- Accumulated Watch Time
- Keyword Relevance

The first thing I look at is keyword relevancy, and I do that by identifying how many of the top twenty video results contain the exact search query in their video title.

In the next image, you'll see that only one video title contains an exact match for the search query "increase YouTube views."

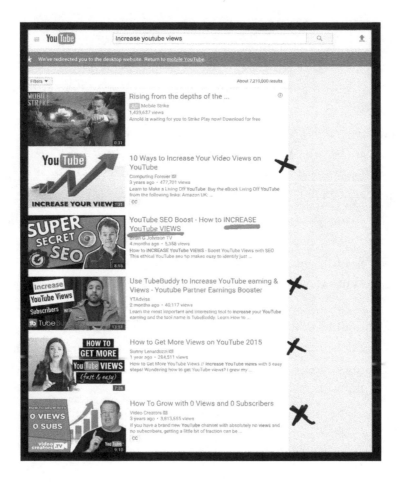

You'll note that my video title **does contain** additional keyword phrases. I added a few more once I saw my audience retention was above average and my video was driving consistent views and thus accumulating watch time. I also look to see if any video has a 100 percent relevancy match, meaning the video title is the exact same as the keyword query. In this case, none of the top nine video results are optimized for relevancy and thus, I'll get a boost. This can be telling when it comes to relevancy. For example, if our keyword query "increase YouTube views" shows up in a video title that contains ten words (including the search query), YouTube considers that to be less relevant than a video title that contains five or six words (including the search query). The shorter the overall title that contains our search terms, the greater relevancy YouTube gives that video in regards to those terms.

Keyword Phrase Prominence

Another thing that YouTube looks at when it comes to relevancy is this: At what point does the keyword query show in the video title? A video title that features the phrase at the beginning of the video rather than at the end would be more relevant.

So, the title "Increase YouTube Views Tutorial" would be considered more relevant than "Tutorial on How to Increase YouTube Views."

Does the Video Title Contain an Exact Match?

Relevance will also be greater if the video title contains the exact keyword phrase in the exact order in which the viewer typed it in.

In our example, the video titled "Trick to Increase YouTube Views" is an exact match because the video title contains the exact keyword query "increase YouTube views."

By contrast, the video entitled "10 Ways to Increase Your Video Views on YouTube" does not contain an exact match, therefore is less relevant, at least according to YouTube's search algorithm.

Does the Video Description Include an Exact Match?

Next, let's look at the video descriptions. Do the top five ranking videos contain an exact keyword match in the first ten words of the video description?

This is especially important when it comes to Google ranking because Google relies much more on text rather than video viewing metrics. It's always smart to include the search phrase you're targeting in the first ten words of your video's description.

iYouTube SERP Study: Video Length, Retention & Accumulated Watch Time

In a recent YouTube SERP (search engine results page) study, YouTube stated, *"We've started adjusting the rankings of videos in YouTube search to reward engaging videos that keep viewers watching."*

Read that again. The part that says *"engaging videos that keep viewers watching"* is important. That's YouTube's way of saying that the longer viewers watch your video (because they find it engaging), the higher it will rank in search.

With that in mind, it makes sense to pay close attention to the length of those videos that are currently ranking for a given keyword query. See the image below for an example.

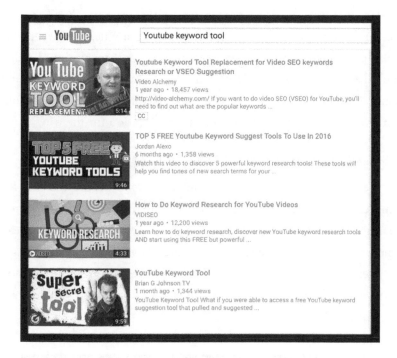

Current Ranking Videos & Video Length

In the previous image, notice that two of the videos in the top four are approximately ten minutes in length, and the other two are four minutes in length. If you publish a four-minute video, it's impossible to keep viewers watching for five minutes (duh).

They can watch for a maximum of four minutes, which means you may not rank as highly as videos of more than four minutes. Keep in mind that video length is directly tied to "accumulated minutes watched."

If a four-minute video has an average view duration of two minutes, one hundred video views would generate two hundred accumulated minutes watched (watch time). However, if a video has an average view duration of five minutes, then that video would generate five hundred accumulated minutes watched (watch time). But wait, there's more!

It's not just how long people watch that matters. YouTube also measures the percentage of people that bail on a video and when they bail. If someone watches two minutes of your four-minute video, YouTube keeps up with that and uses it to rank the video in search results. The lesson is simple: Keep more people watching longer, and you'll win. Viewers plus engagement times duration for the win.

Relative Audience Retention & The First Few Minutes of a Video

Here's another of my super-secret theories. I believe the first few minutes of a video carries much more weight in the YouTube algorithm—and with the viewer—than the last few minutes, so I work hard to create super-engaging content in the first minute or two. If a viewer is engaged early on, chances are greater that they will stick around to watch more of the video. Check out the image on the next page, and you'll see the basis for my theory.

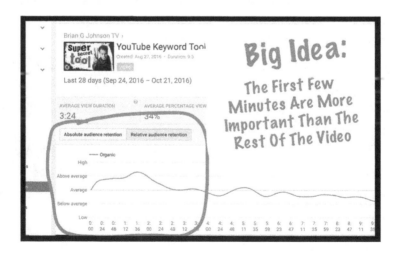

This does not mean that you should simply create longer videos for the sake of increasing watch time. Longer doesn't always mean better when it comes to content and engagement.

If you're just stretching out the length of the video without providing anything of value, the viewer will sense that and move on to something else. And they may not come back ever again if they feel they're being manipulated by you.

I create videos based on the topic that I want to cover without worrying about length. If it takes me two minutes or ten minutes to engage the viewer while getting my point across, so be it. Hopefully, the viewer will find value in the content, like and subscribe to my channel, and come back for more great content another time.

Exact Match Videos & Video Views

Since we know that accumulated watch time and relative audience retention matter in search rankings, it also makes sense to look at how many views the videos have that contain an exact match to the search query in the title. For example, if a video has a keyword phrase exact match, but less than 5,000 views, I know that the video does not carry a high amount of video authority.

Top Ranking Videos & Subscriber Size

It's been shown that, on average, subscribers watch videos longer than nonsubscribers. Therefore, it makes sense to look at the subscriber base of videos that are ranking highly for a particular search query. This is especially true for videos that you can tell have been optimized for search relevancy as discussed on the previous pages. Let's look at how this can play out on YouTube.

The Power of Subscribers: Longer View Duration/Retention

In the following image, notice that the number one "traffic source" for my "Keyword Tool" video is "Suggested Videos," meaning that YouTube has found the video relevant enough that they "suggest" it to viewers watching videos of similar topic.

Notice that the average view duration of "Suggested Videos" is a bit longer than the view duration of the number two traffic source, which is YouTube's general search.

That's probably because the viewers getting those suggestions are already my subscribers watching another of my videos. Subscribers watch more videos, longer—an important point to always remember. The third source of views comes from "browse features," which drives a fair amount of views (18 percent) and this is where things begin to get interesting.

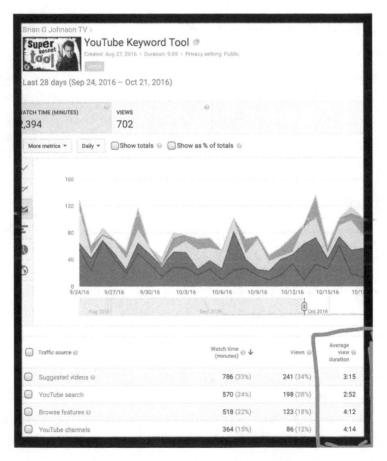

The "average view duration" for browse features is considerably longer. In fact, it's 1:23 seconds longer than views that are driven by general search. That's a third longer average view duration. This, of course, prompts the question: where do "browse feature" views come from and how can I get some more? MOAR!

Click the little question mark next to "browse features" to see the sources of that traffic. The explanation tells you that this traffic comes from the homepage/home screen, the subscription feed, and other browsing features.

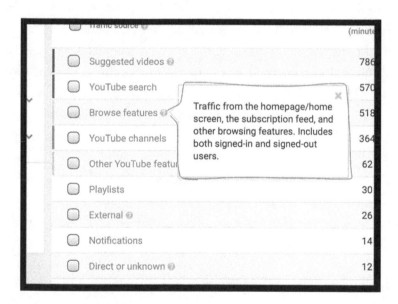

When I go to my YouTube home screen, the video recommendations shown there are videos from channels that I'm subscribed to. So, when one of my subscribers visits their home screen, chances are my videos will appear under recommendations if I've done everything correctly to get my videos ranked in YouTube's system.

As my channel has grown in subscribers over the past seven months or so, this source of views (traffic) has greatly increased.

The Big Idea-Ongoing Subscriber Views

When I first started posting videos on YouTube, I was under the impression that as I published new videos, those videos would be available to subscribers via the subscription feed. They are available; however, YouTube also customizes the homepage and home screen for individual YouTube viewers based on their browsing habits and the channels they're subscribed to. This means that videos you publish will continue to drive "subscriber views" long after your recently published video drops off the subscription feed.

And as I keep saying, subscribers watch longer than nonsubscribers, which results in higher relative audience retention and accumulated watch time. But wait! Yep, there's still more. If you continue adding subscribers as time goes by, you also get a boost from "video view velocity," a YouTube metric that measures how many views a video gets in the first twenty-four to seventy-two hours. Obviously, the more subscribers you have, the more views you should get when you first post a video. Once your channel crosses the 5,000-subscriber mark, you're able to drive more views more quickly. Those with high subscriber numbers like 100,000 or more play an entirely different game than most of us mere mortals. The lesson is this: the more subscribers, the greater your video view velocity.

Video Topics/Keyword Targeting

Engaging content, at least in the sense of YouTube, can best be described as video content that literally causes a person to stop what they're doing and engage (give focus) with the video, and remain engaged for a length of time, hopefully for the entire duration of the video.

It's important that your content is so interesting to your audience that they want to engage with it. Engagement breeds loyalty, so eventually subscribers will look forward to engaging with new content you produce in the future.

We've already established that YouTube puts great emphasis on engaging content because it engages the viewer and makes them watch longer. You have the fish on the hook. Don't let it get away! How do you come up with ideas for engaging content? It's not that difficult once you begin to publish videos on a regular basis. There are several things I do to identify topics that viewers in my target audience might find engaging. Here are a couple of hacks for you.

One: Record as Much as Possible

I research ideas, topics, and keyword phrases on my iPad. When I find something interesting, I create a screen capture and save it to an album in the photos app. Simple and effective.

I also have several whiteboards in my video studio. One is so huge that I also use it to brainstorm playlists and keyword phrase ideas. I begin with the YouTube keyword scroll method (explained below) and simply write down phrase after phrase that I think those in my target audience will find engaging. This is a great way to identify what a market is looking for. For example, I did this with iMovie and came up with at least twenty-five keyword phrase ideas. That resulted in a playlist of about ten videos, which are driving a LOT of views and generating a LOT of subscribers.

YouTube Singular Keyword Scroll Method

The YouTube keyword scroll method is super simple. It's basic, and it works incredibly well. I love simple, it makes it easy for me to move forward! Here's how it works. Go to YouTube and enter in one singular word that best describes a particular topic you think viewers might be interested in.

If the topic generates enough potential keyword phrases, you can then create a playlist around this topic. In the following example, I typed in the singular keyword "iMovie" to discover related search terms

YouTube visitors are searching for. Typically, these first suggestions are the keyword phrases driving the most search volume.

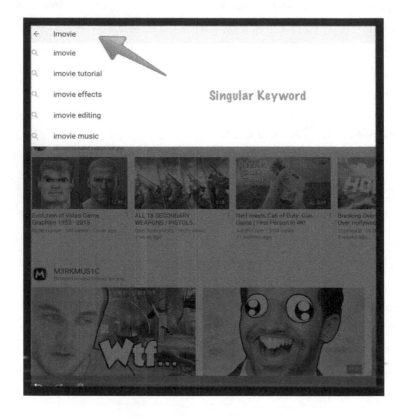

Next, I begin to scroll through the alphabet. This prompts YouTube to display keyword phrases that begin with my seed keyword "iMovie" plus words that begin with each letter of the alphabet.

For example:

- iMovie a
- iMovie b
- iMovie c

Scrolling through the alphabet in this manner produces a crazy amount of potential keyword phrases to target for topics that are popular on YouTube. This is also how I identified one of my first high-ranking keyword phrases: *iMovie App Tutorial*.

This method can be used to identify keyword phrases in any niche, for any subject. You might also start the process with two keyword phrases, rather than one. Instead of just entering "iMovie," enter "iMovie app" and then scroll through the alphabet.

The Think Different Keyword Research Method

One of my favorite keyword research methods is what I call the "think differently" method. The idea is simple. Identify one keyword phrase, such as "iMovie App Tutorial," and then identify what words in the phrase could be substituted to create entirely new keyword phrases.

In the example "iMovie App Tutorial," the word *iMovie* could easily be interchanged with *iPhone/iPad/iPod/iOS*.

So, the search term becomes "*iPad App Tutorial*" or "*iPod App Tutorial.*" Or the word "*App*" could be replaced by another word, for instance like something as simple as "*iMovie iPad Tutorial.*" You get the idea. Taking the time to think through other potential phrases gives you lots of options when it comes to finding good keyword phrases to target. Remember, the goal is to target a phrase that is not as competitive as those in the top search result. In this example, most published videos on the topic of iMovie for mobile were using the words *iPhone/iPad/ iPod/iOS*.

In fact, out of the top twenty or so videos for the phrase "iMovie App Tutorial," only two or three had incorporated the exact phrase into their video titles. So, I used the exact phrase (and only the exact phrase), and sure enough, over the next two weeks, my video began to rise for that keyword phrase.

After a month or so, I was ranking #2 for my target keyword phrase. Later, I added iPhone/iPad and iOS to my title to help my video rank for phrases that contained those words. I could maintain my #2 rankings for iMovie App Tutorial because by this time, I had accumulated watch time and my viewer retention was good.

Channel Identification Method

This is a method that can be used to uncover popular topics as well as keyword phrases that may be worth targeting. The idea was brought to my attention by Brandon Nankivell, who runs a fantastic "book summary" channel on YouTube called "One Percent Better," which may be found at this link:

- https://www.youtube.com/channel/
  UCRI6t05DNVlV0XhdI7hx_iw

Again, the concept is simple. First, go to YouTube and identify channels that cover topics like yours. Next, using the search results "sort" feature, sort their videos based on "popularity." You'll see a list of their videos ranked by popularity. Check out the most popular topics that are getting lots of views and think about doing a video on that topic for your channel.

This method is so easy, so simple, but so very effective. Instead of trying to reinvent the wheel, focus on topics that have already proven to be high rollers (no pun intended) for other channels in your genre. If you hope to build a YouTube channel with lots of subscribers, it's imperative that you create videos that people want to watch, rather than videos you think are cool.

Look at it like a business. Customers want to buy things they like, not things you like. To build an audience (customer base) on YouTube, put yourself in the viewer's place. You succeed by delivering engaging content that you *know* your audience wants, not content you *think* they might want.

Just because you're excited about a potential topic doesn't mean your audience will be. Before you waste a ton of time and effort producing a video, do the keyword research described above to ensure that an audience for that video exists. If you find no keyword search results for the primary keyword for the topic, chances are the only person who will watch that video is you.

SIDE NOTE: Subscribe to channels that focus on topics that are like yours. You may get inspired or come across ideas that you would not have gotten otherwise. Don't copy their videos, but draw inspiration from them. The point is to gain insight into what their viewers are interested in, rather than copying someone's work.

The Just Born Keyword Phrase Method

Search engines are bound to two factors: supply and demand. In the case of YouTube, "supply" refers to the inventory of videos ready to be served up based on search queries. The search queries are the demand. Every day there are new keyword phrases being born and videos created to supply the need.

For example, YouTube is always rolling out new features. Because users want information on how to use these new features, they become powerful keyword search phrases. If your YouTube channel is all about teaching others how to use YouTube, and YouTube introduces a new "clone a poodle" feature, you can learn how the new feature works, then quickly publish a video explaining the new feature before anyone else does. You'll have far less competition for the hot keyword search phrase "YouTube clone poodle feature" because there will be far fewer videos targeting that term. However, within a month, there could be dozens of videos posted on the topic, so it's important that you strike while the iron is hot.

There are keyword phrases that are just being born right now as you read this, as well as authors publishing new books, new products being released, new model numbers, new gadgets, and more.

Balance Your Time the Best You Can

So, there you have it, the super-secret bag of tricks that I use every day to identify high-ranking keywords and search terms. I've had great success with these methods, and you can too. They have allowed me to rank videos high in YouTube search, build lists, and make money to buy lots of food for my poodles.

As you move forward, understand that nothing is more important than uploading another video, then another, and another. I suggest you spend no more than thirty minutes per video on research, then focus on creating great, engaging content. That will give you enough time to identify various phrases, select the one you feel makes the most sense to target, and move on.

Tube Rank Ritual Upload

The following twelve steps are based on the workflow that I use to create, upload, and optimize my videos. These steps were designed to keep the attention on what matters most:

- Identify relevant search terms and topics
- Create engaging videos
- Create engaging thumbnails
- Upload the video and make sure the title and description are optimized
- Rinse and repeat on a consistent basis

One last tip: Publishing regularly to YouTube and doing all these things well takes a fair amount of time and practice. It's not about creating the perfect video with your first few uploads. It's about moving forward and gaining those important skills along the way and striving to improve with each video you upload.

Step 1: Identify the Primary Keyword Phrase Target

These twelve steps divide keyword research into three separate steps. Step 1 is to identify the primary keyword phrase that you'll target. You do this by implementing some of the keyword research methods we covered earlier.

The primary keyword phrase target is one search term that's usually between three and six words long. By identifying one keyword phrase target, we'll be able to optimize the YouTube metadata (video title, description, and tags) based on this one phrase. This is at the core of any solid SEO optimization strategy. As we move forward, we'll use my "YouTube Keyword Tool" video as a case study.

SIDE NOTE: The goal is to identify the keyword phrase that looks to be the easiest to rank for. This is especially true if your channel does not yet have a lot of authority.

In our case study example (following image), you can see I first identified the primary keyword phrase target "YouTube Keyword Tool." Once you've identified your primary keyword target, move on to step two.

Step 2: Identify a Focus Keyword(s) within the Target Search Term

Step 2 allows you to reduce your target keyword phrase, which can often be a longer string of words, into just one word or two. We do this to optimize your video description and tags as well as your video thumbnail.

A quick word about YouTube thumbnails. When creating thumbnails, less is more, and in a very big way. YouTube viewers do not read thumbnails, they *scan* over them, and if your thumbnail fails to *catch their eye*, they'll just keep on going. You'll create your video thumbnail in step six. For now, you simply want to identify the most important two words from within your target keyword phrase. In our case study example, our two words are "keyword tool."

Step 3: The YouTube Video Title Ritual

What's the best way to craft a YouTube video title? That's a question that's impossible to answer without having additional channel data. A brand-new channel that's just been launched has zero published videos and zero *active* subscribers. Thus, you should craft YouTube titles based on the **zero-authority principle**.

However, a channel that is several years old and has published several hundred videos that are driving views and converting viewers into subscribers requires a totally different approach. An established channel with active subscribers is going to be able to drive views within hours of uploading a video, thanks to the subscription feed. And don't forget, views from *Suggested Videos* and *browse features* will also continue to push views weeks and months after publishing.

Statistically speaking, an authoritative channel with active subscribers can publish videos that generate above-average **relative audience retention** as well as accumulated **watch time** metrics, two of the most important aspects of the YouTube search algorithm, with the third being **keyword relevancy**.

So, when it comes to the YouTube video title, more authoritative channels can focus less on relevancy because they're able to generate positive watch time metrics. Channels with less authority should focus more on relevancy, because they're not able to generate as many active subscriber views early on. Here's the good news, **The YouTube Video Title Ritual** makes the process easy, regardless of your channel authority. Just apply the following ritual, and you'll be good to go.

The YouTube Video Title Ritual

A) Primary Keyword Phrase	-	B) Secondary Keyword(s)
No matter what. Begin by selecting and beginning your video title with an exact YouTube keyword phrase.		Add additional keyword(s) if your video or channel has the authority to drive positive watch time metrics.

The Video Title Ritual is based on using an "A and B" tilting system.

A. Begin your title with your Primary Keyword Phrase (this is what you identified in Step 1).
B. Add secondary singular keywords or phrases if:
    1. You have an active subscriber base and you're able to drive views in the first twenty-four hours
    2. Your video is driving consistent views and has accumulated watch time
    3. Your video is driving consistent views and has generated "above average" relative audience retention

For example, if your channel is brand new, then you'd implement Step A and be done. That is, you'd add the exact primary keyword phrase to your title. However, if you have an active subscriber base and can drive views within the first twenty-four hours of uploading, then you may want to implement Step B to incorporate additional keyword phrases or even a secondary phrase. Doing this can potentially help a video rank for additional keyword phrases. Last, you should also revisit videos you published a few months ago to see if they're driving views.

If so, you may want to proceed to Step B with these videos, as well by adding a few additional keyword phrases.

If you're unsure about adding additional keyword phrases at this stage of your YouTube career, I would suggest you simply **stick with Step A**. In our case study example, when I published my "YouTube Keyword Tool" video, I stuck with Step A. However, that may change in the future, because the video is now generating positive watch time metrics.

Step 4: The YouTube Description Ritual

In Step 3, we created a title based on the primary keyword phrase. In Step 4, we'll use the same strategy to craft our description. Begin your description with a sentence that includes your primary keyword phrase.

Next, write a paragraph or two that incorporates additional relevant keyword phrases. We can easily identify additional relevant keyword phrases by simply searching YouTube. If your primary keyword phrase is on the short side, say three or four words, simply search YouTube and make note of the keyword phrases that YouTube suggests.

You can also search YouTube with your focus keyword(s) which you identified in Step 2, as well as any related keyword phrases. The goal here is to get a better idea of the kinds of search terms that YouTube users are searching for when looking for videos similar to what you are uploading.

So, after you've taken a few minutes and performed several keyword searches, write a few additional paragraphs that logically include some of the words that you identified in the various search terms. Keep it simple, and don't spend a ton of time on this because, in the end, the ranking value the description brings to YouTube videos pales in comparison to watch time metrics.

To be clear, the description can and does impact rankings. However, with so much to do, I think it's important that you focus on what is most important and that's to publish another video!

Step 5: The YouTube Meta Tag Ritual

When it comes to YouTube, "meta tags" are singular words or multiword phrases that you add to your video upload data to help YouTube better understand what your video is about and rank it accordingly. This is especially important for new videos because YouTube does not have any analytical data to better understand what your video is about. There are several types of tags that you'll want to add, and they are as follows:

Primary Keyword Phrase Target Tag

This is the target phrase you identified in Step 1. You'll want to add that phrase to your meta tags as an exact match meta tag. If your keyword phrase was "YouTube Keyword Tool," add that exact phrase as a meta tag to the video's listing.

Unique Channel Tag

This is a meta tag that you add to every one of your videos. Doing so can result in more of your own videos showing up in YouTube Suggested Videos. I use my channel name, with and without spaces, like this:

- brian g johnson tv/briangjohnsontv

YouTube Long Tail Search Terms

Creating additional meta tags based on keyword stemming is powerful. Keyword stemming is simply a keyword phrase that's based on the original phrase. You dig? For example, if our primary keyword phrase is "YouTube Keyword Tool," then I would simply enter that into YouTube to identify any additional phrases that might stem from this original phrase. Notice the screen capture image below and the four black arrows that highlight *stemmed keyword phrases*.

Step 6: Create a Thumbnail That Incorporates the Focus Keyword Method

Thumbnails are critically important to YouTube success because thumbnails are the first points of engagement between you and prospective viewers. If your thumbnail catches their eye, i.e., engages them, the odds that they will click to view your video increase exponentially. So, you should allocate a good bit of your time to creating engaging, awesome, eye-catching thumbnails. I'll often tweak a thumbnail several times before I feel that I've created something that truly pops. Keep in mind that thumbnails are not set in stone. You can tweak and change a thumbnail anytime you like. I have several older thumbnails that I may change at some point. In the coming pages, I've included a few tips that will teach you how to craft simple, elegant, less-is-more thumbnails.

Playlist Thumbnail Templates & Themes

Be consistent in the design of your thumbnails and other YouTube graphic elements. To build a recognizable brand, create playlist thumbnail themes that include the same color palettes, words, imagery, style, graphical elements (such as an icon or logo) and font. Congruency is a powerful element that naturally draws the eye and thus will help you grab more attention.

One: Less Is More

Your number one goal should be to make it as easy as possible for YouTube viewers to find and subscribe to your channel. That's why a consistency of design and clarity of branding are so important. A minimalistic thumbnail is far easier for the brain to process and understand. And if all your thumbnails are similar in design and style, they'll know it's *you* right out of the gate.

Thumbnail Focus Word(s) Ritual

Implement the thumbnail focus word ritual by selecting the most critical word or two from your primary keyword phrase target. Remember, adding the entire primary keyword phrase to a thumbnail can result in a busy, harder to comprehend thumbnail. Also, you may want to add an additional word or two that results in an enticing phrase, which in turn can absolutely result in more clicks. Over the last handful of months, I have created bigger and bigger words, pushing the words up into the border to increase the size. I believe this results in my thumbnails grabbing attention more quickly. As mentioned previously, check my channel on YouTube to see how my thumbnails stand out and pop.

For my "YouTube Keyword Tool" video, I created a thumbnail that included two words NOT present in my primary keyword phrase: super secret. The resulting phrase of "super-secret tool" is spot-on and works well when combined with the video title.

Step 7: Add Needed YouTube Cards

Next, you'll want to add any needed YouTube end cards to your video. If you referenced a YouTube video and/or a playlist in your video, add an end card that links to the appropriate video or playlist.

If your goal is to drive viewers to your associated website to build a list and/or sell a product, then always include a card that links to the appropriate page.

Step 8: Add Your YouTube End Screen

As I write this on October 27, the YouTube end screen feature has just been rolled out to all channels. That makes it super-easy to add an end card to all your videos. This works best if you end your videos with a twenty second or less call to action. Your call to action will be based on your overall goals for that video. As mentioned previously, my verbal call to action will always be to "subscribe for more videos."

I will also add an end screen element to build my list, thus I will incorporate a "Free eBook" call to action or something similar. Last, remember you need to add at least one video or a playlist to an end screen to prompt the viewer to keep watching your videos.

Step 9: Ritual Rank Velocity Tactic

The YouTube algorithm measures the number of views a video gets in the first twenty-four to seventy-two hours. Therefore, a video that drives more views on the first few days tells YouTube that the video is engaging and deserves a higher rank in the search results.

To help get more views during these critical first few days, you should promote your video starting the second after you hit the publish button.

Here is my workflow:

1. Share to Facebook (personal and group pages)
2. Share to Twitter
3. Email my list

Doing this has helped me drive more views quicker, and this positively impacts the algorithm in many ways. If you're thinking, *Gosh, Brian has a list, and I can't get the results he did,* then understand that that, my friend, is not true. I can guarantee you that if I had no list, or authority at all, I would still succeed on YouTube. How would I do it?

I would implement the very **Tube Ritual 30-Day Challenge** you are reading about right this second. By publishing lots of simple, engaging videos over a short time, I could build my channel to thousands of subscribers in just a few months and so can you. I've worked with coaching clients who were under the impression that success on YouTube stems from external promotion and video syndication. It's true, having big websites embed your video can greatly improve overall results without question. However, to make that happen, you need to publish an awesome—and I mean awesome—video.

How do you publish an awesome video? By practicing the art of video creation and marketing. That's why this book and the ritual it covers is so powerful.

If you build it, will they come?

Only if you market wisely.

And if they come, will they stay?

Only if you engage them once they're there. In the end, create great content and great things will happen. You dig?

Step 10: Comment & Engage with Subscribers

"People won't care how much you know until they know how much you care."

That's a popular quote that's been attributed to Teddy Roosevelt and John C. Maxwell, among others. I don't care who first said it. I just know that it's spot-on.

Those YouTubers who understand that engagement goes beyond the thumbnail and video are the ones who do amazingly well. Engagement includes soliciting and replying to comments for every video you publish. Gary Vaynerchuk, who swears like a sailor and is a bit of an acquired taste, takes the time to reply to viewers who comment on his threads. If someone takes the time to leave you a comment, which can improve your channel growth, I suggest you take the time to thank them, answer their question, or simply engage with them by saying thanks for stopping by.

I do my best to reply to probably about 97 percent of those who comment on my channel. Of course, it gets harder and harder as you grow and more and more comments are left. But do your best, and your subscribers will respect you for it.

Step 11: Study Past Video Performance "RELATIVE AUDIENCE RETENTION"

I believe in the power of repetition. I said . . . I believe in the power of repetition. That's why I've mentioned those things that I feel are important several times. I've mentioned again and again the importance of engagement, which can be measured by relative audience retention inside your YouTube analytics dashboard. While some people find analytics boring, I find them to be extremely important because they tell you what's working and what's not.

For example, log in to your YouTube control panel and study the relative audience retention of your last few videos. What does the data tell you? If you don't know, don't worry. Learning to understand analytics is another of those things you'll do over time.

Get into the habit of checking your analytics regularly for things like relative audience retention. It will help you learn a great deal about how your audience perceives your videos. Just remember this: **Nothing is more important than retention**. Not the keywords, not the thumbnails, or any other bit of metadata. Audience retention is the foundation upon which you'll build your empire on YouTube. You can study the relative audience retention of your videos by logging into YouTube, then select:

1. Video manager (Inside Creator Studio)
2. Click the video title link
3. Click the "Analytics" button below the video
4. Click "Average View Duration"
5. Click "Relative Audience Retention"

Step 12: Ponder Your Next Video Upload

Going through these twelve steps takes a bit of time, but there's no better way to learn how to come up with engaging video topics, improve your on-camera skills and editing style, improve thumbnail creation, and more. You now know how to research popular keyword phrases, and in the process, you'll no doubt run across dozens of ideas for videos that you could start creating right away. You understand the importance of replying to comments, which can also be a great source for video ideas.

Last, you learned the importance of studying your analytics to gain insight into what your audience likes and what they don't like. Don't be intimidated by the next video. Look forward to it because each video you create takes you closer to your goal of having a killer YouTube channel.

Get Integrated!

Integrate My 12-Step YouTube

Checklist Right into the
YouTube Upload Dashboard
with TubeBuddy! (Free Software) and

YouTube Starter Kit

Access: BrianGJohnson.TV/Free

THE LAST WORD

When you **#StakeYourClaim** and decide to do something, that is not to hope, want, or wonder. But rather, decide that you'll do the thing and you'll give it your all. Do that, and you'll succeed again and again.

Apply this mentality to the Tube Ritual 30-Day Challenge, and you'll succeed in numerous ways—that is, if you truly apply yourself. It doesn't matter if you miss a day or make a few mistakes along the way. That's bound to happen, but in the process you'll discover what you're made of and you'll have created a body of work that may be imperfect, but that you're proud of.

Mark My Words

Many people will read this book, some of whom will apply the strategies and tactics found within. As these individuals reach the last few days of their own personal Tube Ritual Challenges, they'll be amazed at the growth in views and subscribers, not to mention the personal satisfaction of doing something worthwhile. Will you be one of those individuals?

I dare ya.

Brian G. Johnson

*People **DO NOT** fail, they simply **GIVE UP***

before the magic happens.

#StakeYourClaim
#AmplifyYourMessage
#InspireAction

Morgan James
Speakers Group

www.TheMorganJamesSpeakersGroup.com

We connect Morgan James published
authors with live and online events
and audiences who will benefit
from their expertise.